WHY DO NUMBERS COUNT

by

Lance Shaler

Copyright © 2010 by Lance Shaler

All rights reserved. No part of this book may be reproduced or transmitted in any form or by any means, electronic or mechanical, including photocopying, recording, or by an information storage and retrieval system, without permission in writing from the publisher.

Published by:

Lance Shaler
Sci-Com Data Services Ltd.
402 – 1488 Hornby Street
Vancouver, B.C. V6Z 1X3
www.numbers-count.com

Logo Trademark TMA369,120 by Lance Shaler

ISBN 978-0-9866217-2-7

1. Family 2. Relationships 3. Self Help 4. Spirituality
5. Psychology

Cover Art & Illustrations by Eve Lees
evelees@telus.net
www.artnews-healthnews.com

Book Design by Lance Shaler
lance@numbers-count.com
www.numbers-count.com

Printed in USA
2010 1st Printing

BOOK COVER

The book cover depicts numbers as a common thread weaving themselves throughout the universe. The background stars are the Pleiades, also known as the Seven Sisters.

Why Do Numbers Count

DEDICATED TO:

A WORLD WHERE

MEN AND WOMEN

ACCEPT EACH OTHER

FOR BEING WHO THEY ARE...

A WORLD IN WHICH PEOPLE

CELEBRATE THEIR DIFFERENCES

QUOTES

In the 10 years that I have known Lance Shaler, he has always made Numbers Count for himself and others. I have truly learned a great deal from him, and I recommend him to you.

Chuck Spezzano, Ph.D., MCFC, psychotherapist

Simple, clear, undiluted and haunting. Each page demanded that I read the next one.

Les Atchison, C.A., professional accountant

Wow!! And I thought that I wasn't interested in numerology.

Laura Larkin, Ph.D, Humanities, counsellor

This is more than a book on numerology, it is a vibrant expression of the author's love for humankind and the planet. This book gave me hope that a more loving world is possible.

Joan Sutton-Brown, L.L.B., lawyer

What a wonderful relief to discover so many reasons for me being the way I am. I'm grateful for the peace this book has given me. Thank you.

Sabrina Braham, M.A., MCFC,
psychotherapist, author

I've always wanted to learn numerology, but didn't have the energy to wade through all the data. This book made it fun and easy. Exceptionally well done!!

Kelly Henderson, BSN, R.N., registered nurse

It's uncanny how Lance can pinpoint my personal cycles down to specific days. He's so clear that sometimes I feel like he was there with me. I listen very carefully when he talks of my future.

Robert-Michael Kaplan, O.D., M.Ed.,
author & vision educator

I don't run my life by numerology or astrology but I love to feel their influences. This book brings me great joy and more connection to the mystery that I love.

Paulette Tomasson, RN, RCC, MA,
Nurse Counsellor

This is a book that will never gather dust on my shelf, will never go into storage. It will sit at my side and will have a certain patina to it – just like my connection to the author. His insight leaves me speechless – and that's not common for me! He's gifted me with wings and I can fly.

Rev. Karey Sinclaire (formerly Rev. Carrie Hunter)

I've known Lance for many years, including we worked on more than one project together. Both in business and personally, I frequently watched him do his magic with numbers. Without question, he is "Mr. Numerology".

Sam Adams, Master Distributor, Amega Global

This book reads more like a novel than a text. Great job!!

Doug Campbell, B.Arch, architect

Credible, inviting and reassuring.

Rico Ricketts, B.Sc., D.M.D., dentist

ACKNOWLEDGEMENTS

Numerology appears to be as old as time itself. Pythagoras of Samos, known as the Father Of Numerology, acquired his initial insights from the Egyptians about 600 B.C. The symbology of numbers is common to most mythologies, religions, and oracles such as the tarot, astrology, and the I Ching.

For example, in Christianity, the days of creation reflect the qualities of numbers, the Old Testament contains a Book Of Numbers, the Baptism asks, "*Who gave this child this name, and what will this name do for this child*?" In Revelations, "*One is given a white stone. Within the white stone is inscribed a new name only to be known unto oneself.*" In Christianity, there are many name changes such as "*Saul changed his name to Paul and he became ... Sarai to Sarah and she became*". The Jewish Kabbalah is infused with numerological references as is the Order of Rosicrucians and Freemasonry.

To specifically acknowledge each person and event which has contributed to this book would be quite impossible. However, it is important for me to acknowledge the ancients for their wisdom and all those who build on their foundation through to this present era of insight and radical change.

Within our changing world, this book speaks of my conviction that life has purpose, meaning, and an inherent design — that life is not a random happenstance of unrelated events. I believe that the people of this planet will become increasingly willing to embrace reasonable solutions as the conscious awareness of hope, purpose, and the inherent design of life become more apparent. As we become progressively more responsible for our environment, both personally and globally, we will establish a sustainable future.

Although the ideas of this book are only one piece of the huge puzzle of life, for the picture to be complete, all pieces of the puzzle must be included in appropriate perspective.

Why Do Numbers Count

Specifically, I want to acknowledge all those who for years pestered me to write this book and encouraged me to pursue what I love to do. For their loving support, I acknowledge Desiree Panico, Dawn Macaskill, Paulette Tomasson, Donalei Tabak, Lesley Tomlin, Joan Sutton-Brown, Carol Johnson, Les Atchison, Chuck Spezzano, Nancy Shipley Rubin, Cynthia deHay, Terry & Athena Ferguson, Glenn Urquhart, Steffany Caldwell, Andy Bryce, Andy Mar, Teya Danel, Robert-Michael Kaplan, and Donna Johnson. Plus a special thank you to my Mother for her words of encouragement.

For her impeccable editing and enduring support, a special thank you to Karmel Shaler. For their editorial comments and honesty, I acknowledge Kelly Henderson, Debrah Rafel, Rae Armour, Sabrina Braham, and John Clancy.

For their help on the astrology metaphors, I wish to thank Loralee Scaife, James Mainard, and notably my friend Debra Silverman for her enthusiastic help and brilliant insights.

I thank everyone who has read this book and is searching to understand life's purpose.

TABLE OF CONTENTS

PART I 1
INTRODUCTION 1
    WHAT IS NUMEROLOGY? 2
        Cymatics – Frequency and Form 2
        Symbology and Names 5
        Why Numbers? 6
        Identity and Names 7
    WHAT VALUE WILL YOU DERIVE FROM THIS BOOK? 8
    HOW TO USE THIS BOOK 10
    ABOUT THE AUTHOR 12

PART II 15
QUALITIES OF THE NUMBERS 15
    CHAPTER 1 — QUALITIES OF THE ONE 17
    CHAPTER 2 — QUALITIES OF THE TWO 27
    CHAPTER 3 — QUALITIES OF THE THREE 39
    CHAPTER 4 — QUALITIES OF THE FOUR 47
    CHAPTER 5 — QUALITIES OF THE FIVE 55
    CHAPTER 6 — QUALITIES OF THE SIX 63
    CHAPTER 7 — QUALITIES OF THE SEVEN 69
    CHAPTER 8 — QUALITIES OF THE EIGHT 79
    CHAPTER 9 — QUALITIES OF THE NINE 87
    CHAPTER 10 — POSITIVE VERSUS NEGATIVE TRAITS ... 94
    CHAPTER 11 — METAPHORS & KEYWORDS 97

PART III 105
THE 9 YEAR CYCLE OF LIFE 105
    CHAPTER 12 — THE 9 YEAR CYCLE IN SUMMARY 106
        COMPUTING YOUR CYCLE YEAR 107
        THE 9 YEAR CYCLE OF GROWTH 109
        THE 9 YEAR CYCLE IN SUMMARY 111
        UNSETTLED VS PROGRESSIVE PERIODS 115
    CHAPTER 13 — THE 9 YEAR CYCLE IN DETAIL 117

PART IV **135**

NAME COMBINATIONS **135**

    CHAPTER 14 — COMPUTING NAME COMBINATIONS 136
    CHAPTER 15 — NAMES WITH A 6 SOURCE NUMBER 141
    CHAPTER 16 — NAMES WITH A 6 EXPRESSION NUMBER 150
    CHAPTER 17 — ALL POSSIBLE NAME COMBINATIONS 160
        COMBINATIONS WITH A SOURCE NUMBER OF 1 .... *162*
        COMBINATIONS WITH A SOURCE NUMBER OF 2 .... *169*
        COMBINATIONS WITH A SOURCE NUMBER OF 3 .... *176*
        COMBINATIONS WITH A SOURCE NUMBER OF 4 .... *182*
        COMBINATIONS WITH A SOURCE NUMBER OF 5 .... *187*
        COMBINATIONS WITH A SOURCE NUMBER OF 6 .... *193*
        COMBINATIONS WITH A SOURCE NUMBER OF 7 .... *199*
        COMBINATIONS WITH A SOURCE NUMBER OF 8 .... *207*
        COMBINATIONS WITH A SOURCE NUMBER OF 9 .... *213*

PART V **219**

ANALYZING NAMES & BIRTHDATES **219**

    CHAPTER 18 — HOW TO ANALYZE ALL YOUR NAMES 220
    CHAPTER 19 — BIRTHDATES & THE INNER SELF 224
    CHAPTER 20 — RESOLVING ALL THE NUMBERS 231

PART VI **237**

CHANGING NAMES **237**

    CHAPTER 21 — BEFORE YOU CHANGE ANY NAMES 238
    CHAPTER 22 — BALANCED NAME COMBINATIONS 240

PART VII **245**

SPECIAL TOPICS **245**

    CHAPTER 23 — RELATIONSHIPS & COMPATIBILITY 246
    CHAPTER 24 — HEALTH CONSIDERATIONS & NUMBERS 251
    CHAPTER 25 — BUSINESS MANAGEMENT, MONEY & YOU ... 256

IN CONCLUSION **263**

APPENDICIES **267**

    APPENDIX "A" — THE EVOLUTION OF THE ZODIAC SIGNS 268
    APPENDIX "B" — SUMMARY OF METAPHORS & KEYWORDS 274
    APPENDIX "C" — PROBABILITIES OF SUCCESS 277

NUMBERS **281**

Why Do Numbers Count

PART I

INTRODUCTION

WHAT IS NUMEROLOGY?

Cymatics – Frequency and Form

Cymatics, commonly called "visible sound", is a study that demonstrates how frequency affects matter and creates form. Although names generate a sound when spoken and hence have a relationship to form, I suggest the relationship of a name's frequency affects form at levels deeper than the spoken word.

The relationship of frequency to form is all encompassing and can be found throughout life from the patterns on butterfly wings, bird feather designs, tortoise shells and to the basic structure and design of all life forms.

To view the relationship of frequency and form, Google "Cymatics" and watch some of the videos noted below or peruse some of the books on the topic.

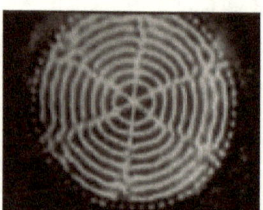

http://www.youtube.com/watch?v=oCmGjD9j9bU&feature=related

http://www.youtube.com/watch?v=bxV0FrFMxUY&feature=related

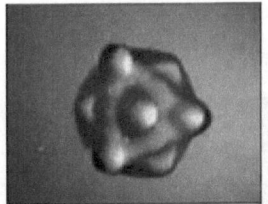

http://www.youtube.com/watch?v=fCXZF3NiPIk&feature=related

http://www.youtube.com/watch?v=EQPMhwuYMy4&NR=1

Forms become more explicit as frequency increases.

For example, the following snapshots are very reflective of a *dragon fly* and *brain coral*.

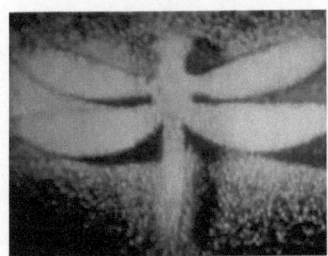 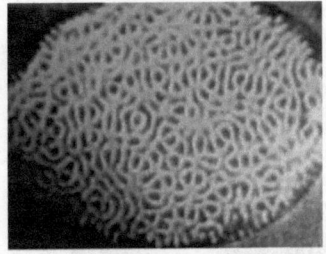

http://www.youtube.com/watch?v=05lo6lop3mk&feature=related

Why Do Numbers Count

The following images, © Dan Blore, can be found at www.cymatics.org

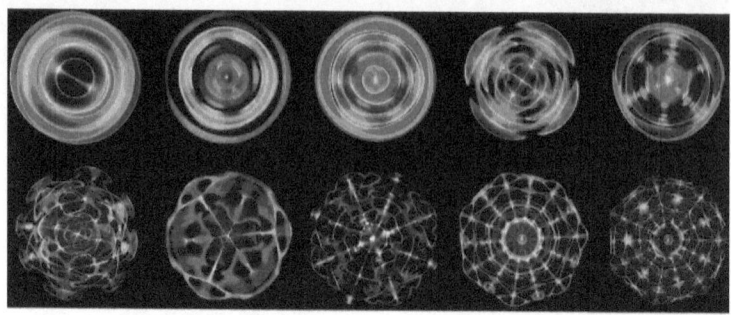

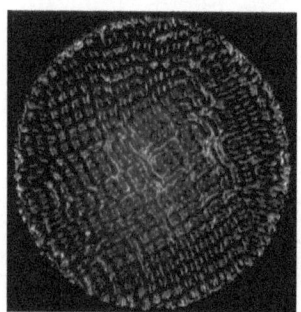

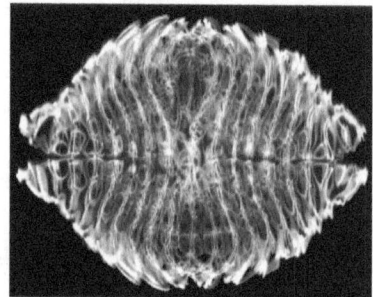

You may also wish to explore: http://cymaticsource.com/ and http://cymatica.net/

An interesting book to consider is:

Cymatics: A Study of Wave Phenomena by Hans Jenny

Symbology and Names

Written language is a very recent development in the evolution of human consciousness. The earliest forms of written language were pictures directly representing things and events — known as pictographs. In some ways, pictographs are similar to the oriental form of logograms. The distinct disadvantage of these systems is the huge number of symbols which must be memorized in order to become literate. For example, one must master a minimum of 3,000 logograms to be minimally literate, and over 50,000 to be fully literate.

The Sumerians' addition of phonetic elements around 3800 B.C. was a vital and progressive step towards simplifying the complexity of written language. Three thousand years later, the Greeks added vowels to the Sumerians' symbols which gave birth to the alphabet proper. While it was considered to take 20 years to fully master the system of logograms, the addition of the vowels by the Greeks reduced the learning period to 3 years. This remarkable contribution occurred about 800 B.C.

In our familiarity with written language, we forget that each letter of an alphabet was chosen to **symbolically** represent and communicate a specific conscious intention. We overlook that words are a precise combination of letters each designed to symbolically communicate their own unique meaning, flavour, tone and quality of intelligence.

The fundamental point is that all words, in every language, are symbolic representations of emotions and concepts. **Unfortunately, we cease to apply the same recognition to people's names.**

One objective of this book is to demonstrate that your name has a symbolic meaning that can be identified by applying numbers to names. Your name embraces specific attitudes, beliefs and feelings which have a dramatic effect on your personhood, including your physical, emotional, mental and spiritual health.

This book is **not** intended to promote that everyone rush out and change their name. Rather, the intention is to point out that each of your names has a direct and specific impact on your character and your life's experience. For those interested, the topic of changing names is addressed at the end of the book in Chapters 21 & 22.

Why Numbers?

Numbers do not have intrinsic powers that dictate specific consequences any more than the words written on this page do. They are convenient, *symbolic* representations of parts of the whole cosmology of life. Although other symbols have a broader universal import than numbers, the numbers 1 to 9 form a primary logic set that are common to most languages of our world.

Imagine a triangular prism that separates white light into the colors of the rainbow. Similarly, imagine the numbers from 1 to 9 within the prism and diffusing the full spectrum of the qualities of life into 9 separate categories. In this sense, numbers are referred to as the grandparent of all the various oracles such as astrology, the tarot, the I-Ching, etc. As such, they are more generalized in their definition, whereas the details of astrology are extensive, indeed.

As the grandparent of all the oracles, the qualities of the numbers are common to most of the world's mythologies, religions and philosophies which affords another good reason to become familiar with the symbology of numbers.

Identity and Names

Your name is like a mantra, a rhythmic chant that you use in your mind, possibly, hundreds of times every day. It is like a tuning fork that each of us takes note of and responds to in accordance with the intensity and degree of chord or 'dischord' that the set of symbols invoke.

Consider a set of piano keys — would you choose a harmonious chord, a semitone or a complete discord of sound to reverberate throughout your entire being dozens of times per day? Or, imagine that every time someone says your name or you think of yourself consciously or unconsciously, your name resonates like squeaky chalk on a blackboard. How long would it take before you would become irritable? After several years, what would be the cumulative effect of hearing such an irritable sound hundreds of times a day? Just because you get used to the road noise, doesn't mean that the constant drone is not wearing on the emotions and the body.

Your name is possibly the most important source of your identity. Most people, when asked "*Who are you?*" respond by giving their name. If you think you are not attached to your name, take a moment and consider changing your name to something completely different. Seemingly from out of nowhere, the "*hums and haws*" begin and it becomes apparent that people are very attached to their names, identifying strongly with what they are called.

In short, your names are very important to you and you consciously and unconsciously identify strongly with them. In addition, their symbolic resonance has outstanding impact on your character and your life's experience. This book can help you understand that impact and substantiate many of your own personal insights and awareness of yourself.

WHAT VALUE WILL YOU DERIVE FROM THIS BOOK?

1. By analyzing the numerical value of names and birthdates, numerology offers a simple, yet, profound insight into the psychology of human nature.

   This book will help you better understand yourself, your children, your parents and your friends. It will complement your perception of the overall cosmology of life and will greatly enhance your sense of compassion for yourself and others.

   The primary value of numerology, over other measuring systems of human nature, is the simplicity of the calculations and the ease of interpreting the ensuing number combinations. To use numerology effectively in personal or business life, one does not require extensive training.

2. A salient feature of this book is identifying the nature of our Inner Selves. This is a quality of one's being that is often buried under many layers of social sanctions that dictate how each of us are *supposed to be*. Our names contribute to our outer persona and can be in direct contradiction to our inner nature. Sometimes we can hear faint, obscure whispers that call us to a different destiny. Yet, without some form of confirmation, it can be impossible to be confident that the whispers are our own. This book helps people identify their true inner nature and offers people permission to be themselves. Coming to grips with the differences between our inner desires and our outer persona can be a life changing experience in itself.

3. Sometimes people cannot relate to the influence of their names or to the nature of their Inner Self. Even so, everyone seems to be able to recognize the influence of the 9 Year

Cycle of Growth that impacts the quality of our lives on a yearly, monthly, and daily basis. Frequently, people will burst into tears when I describe the influence of the cycles on their current experience. It can be a dramatic relief to discover that one's experience is part of the natural pulsation of life rather than the beginning of failing health, financial burdens, relationship problems, etc. It also can be financially rewarding to understand when to invest and when to sell.

4. Why do we get along with some people and not others? Why do some marriages last and others fail? Some answers to these questions are offered in a chapter entitled *Relationships & Compatibility*. The insights of this chapter are useful both to the business executive interested in a well-run company and to people considering long-term relationships. And, it can be fun simply to understand why your best friend is your best friend.

5. In addition to personal names, number combinations have a strong influence on business and product names. The date of incorporation of a business sets the business into a particular year of the 9 Year Cycle. The influence of name combinations is often apparent in the names of cities and countries. Even street numbers on houses and businesses have an influence. These considerations are discussed in the later chapters of the book.

HOW TO USE THIS BOOK

This book divides the nature of life into 9 distinct categories as identified in the first 9 chapters. The characteristics and qualities of each category are symbolized by the numbers 1 through 9 and are referred to as the qualities of the numbers. In an effort to identify the raw energy behind each number, the qualities of the numbers are stereotyped to capture their essence. Later in the book, the dissected parts are brought back to a forum of wholeness and it is acknowledged that each of us is a tapestry of many factors. No one is simply a specific number or a single name.

This book has been written with the assumption that the reader will begin with this introduction and read each chapter sequentially. Each chapter builds and interlinks to the previous one. This is particularly true in Part II of the book which outlines the qualities of the numbers with references to the developmental phases of human growth — infant, child, adolescent, etc. If it is your style to read chapters at random, then it is important to keep in mind that one developmental phase is not better than another. Neither are you simply one number or only your name. Whatever numbers you discover you are, the numbers will identify the style, the tone and the flavour of how you pursue your life, rather than the evolutionary status or the *quantity* of what you can or have achieved.

This book identifies the qualities of the numbers by employing four metaphors: people, plants, senses and astrology. From the interplay of the four stories, basic patterns emerge that create a foundation on which you can build a system of esoteric knowledge as expansive as you personally desire.

Some people find it impossible to read the first 9 chapters without first knowing which overall number they are. If you are one of those people, please turn to Chapter 19 and the section titled **Lifepath** to compute your overall birthdate number.

As you read the first 9 chapters, remember that you are much more than one, single number. All of your names are part of your character as are the month, day, and year of your birth.

So now, sit back and enjoy the first 9 chapters before you consider the application of numbers to names and birthdates. First, you must allow the metaphors to build relationships and word pictures, then the application of numbers will fall into a natural perspective.

ABOUT THE AUTHOR

I spent the last 40 years of my career as the CEO and/or President of a number of companies determining what was real and what was not. Time and again, scepticism proved to be a valuable ally although I found it needs to be partnered with an open mind and a willingness to embrace new ideas.

Turning the clock back, I was introduced to numerology in 1969 by a friend who had a reputation for going from one strange encounter to the next. He was passionately enthralled with his latest discovery, and I decided to acquire some background information to effectively counter his arguments. At the time, I was teaching computer technology, having come from an educational background in electronics, industrial process controls and the advanced technological measurement of physical phenomena. At the time, I believed the universe ran strictly on known scientific law.

When I signed up for an introductory course, my intention was to acquire sufficient knowledge to invalidate numerology and therefore rescue my friend from another of his hare-brained ideas.

I studied with vigour and each time I believed I had found a loophole, I challenged my instructor who patiently pointed out the fallacies of my logic. After six months of concerted effort to invalidate numerology, I reluctantly decided to change my attitude and adopt a more positive approach.

It's now more than 40 years since I was introduced to numerology and it has been the core measuring stick of my life and an exceptionally helpful tool for investigating other belief systems. Seldom is there a day when I don't counsel at least one person on their life's experience based on the tools of numerology. Each day offers me deeper insights into the process of life through the metaphor of numbers.

Even so, sometimes I get obstinate and decide that I am allowing numbers and the natural cycles articulated by numerology to dictate my life. At such times, I say "*To heck with numerology, I'm going to do it anyway*". Those times have fostered the major losses of my life. Slowly I'm becoming more accepting of life and allowing it to be the way it is rather than the way I think it's supposed to be.

During my early studies of numerology, I was plagued with the desire to make the process of learning it more inviting and credible. I'm grateful for the opportunity to share my insights with you.

PART II

QUALITIES OF THE NUMBERS

Some people find it impossible to read this section without first knowing which overall number they are. If you are one of those people, please turn to Chapter 19 and the section titled **Lifepath** to compute your overall birthdate number.

As you read the next 9 chapters, remember that you are much more than one, single number. All of your names are part of your character as are the month, day and year of your birth. Enough said, turn the page and let's get started.

CHAPTER 1 — QUALITIES OF THE ONE

Within the four metaphors, the qualities of the ONE are:

PEOPLE	PLANTS	SENSES	ASTROLOGY
MAN	SEED	TOUCH	ARIES

PEOPLE METAPHOR: MAN

The most obvious physical distinction of man from woman is the genitals. The male genitals are external, they protrude, and their basic function is to ejaculate and impregnate. Ejaculation is an outward projection of energy. Impregnation triggers the process of conception. It's the woman who does the true magic of creating a child and giving birth to a whole new concept of child. Yet, it's the male who triggers the process, begins the process, and then remains separate from the nine month growth cycle.

And so it is that the qualities of the number *one* are like those of the male energy. The *one* is interested in physical, external things. The energy of the *one* projects outward and is invested in beginning new ventures, new ideas, but is not interested in completing projects. For example, the *one* initiates conception but does not incubate or give birth to the child. The male attitude is typically invested in separation, independence, self-sufficiency, whereas the female instinct moves toward fusion, bonding, and resolving the boundaries that separate people.

KEY IMAGE: PIONEER

A poignant image that captures the essence of the number *one* is the pioneer. Consider the qualities of the pioneer in the days of the settlers: independent, self-sufficient, sturdy, strong. Certainly, pioneers are not gregarious, cosmopolitan people who love to socialize and chitchat or they wouldn't be trappers in the mountains or explorers striving to find mountain passages.

How did pioneers dress? One sturdy buckskin outfit and that's it! Likewise, people strong in the *one* quality in our late 20th century do not have large wardrobes. Whatever they have is durable and, if colored, the garment will be a strong color. Women with a predominance of the *one* quality in their nature hate to wear dresses or anything frilly. They love to wear pants, particularly blue jeans. They prefer sturdy shoes, if not boots, rather than high-heeled shoes.

What did the pioneer eat and how often? They ate beef jerky or at least the basics of bread, meat, and potatoes — something practical that sticks to their ribs and offers enough nourishment for a full day's work or journey.

How did pioneers walk? If you had to walk from the east coast of North America to the west coast, you probably would walk with determination taking the shortest possible distance between two points. People strong in the *one* quality have a tendency to walk into parked cars, sleeping dogs, and other stationary objects. They cross busy streets without looking and tend to bang the extremities of  their bodies, namely their toes, fingers, and head. *Ones* are very uni-directional — once their minds are set, they go straight after the person, place, or thing that they want. Their basic style is like a steamroller that stops for nobody or 'no-thing'.

It is virtually impossible to change their minds once they have made a decision. Conversely, they don't make snap decisions, except in the case of survival when they are the experts and utterly pragmatic. Present *ones* with a new idea and they will always have to go away and think it over. Several days later they will return to tell you of the brilliant idea they have worked out. When you point out they are repeating your idea, they will deny you had anything to do with their new concept and claim total ownership, completely oblivious, and utterly insensitive to the suggestion that you had presented them with the idea only three days prior.

Ones are not prone to reason why. They are doers, action people, and very creative at beginning new ventures. They are particularly creative with their hands. *Ones* instinctively take charge of small groups if an accident occurs. Conversely, they shy away from large groups.

Pioneers speak directly and to the point. They call a spade a spade and not a garden implement. They speak only when it is necessary to cover specific, practical details. Consequently, they are factual, unemotional, blunt, and very honest. They call it as they see it and tend to blurt out their opinion without any sense of diplomacy or tact.

What kind of automobile would you expect a *one* to drive? Probably a truck, or if they do drive a car, it's a heavy, sturdy car with no more than an AM radio, if it has any options at all.

What kind of furniture would you expect a *one* to have? Would you expect delicate French Provincial with detailed scrolls everywhere, or would you expect to see a solid oak kitchen table that other people would use for an outdoor picnic table? Whatever it is, it will be sturdy and built to last.

And so the story goes and you can begin to answer your own questions about the qualities of the *one*. Would the pioneer prefer to drink from a mug or a tea cup?

The mug, of course. Likely the mug would not have a handle, or if it does, ones may not even bother to use the handle.

Ones are lean and sinuous in build. They are unbelievably strong for being basically skin, bones, and tendons. Typically, they are big boned and have large feet and hands. They are either bald as can be or have exceptionally thick hair. Bald or not, they have lots of body hair. Their eyes are often recessed, well protected by thick eyebrows and a protruding brow.

They love dairy products such as milk and cheese which they consume to excess producing an abundance of mucus in their system. As a result, they suffer from their fair share of common colds which settle in the head and sinus areas rather than in the throat and chest.

Ones make great friends because they are durable, reliable, solid in their position, and don't change their minds easily. They don't make friends readily, but once they do, a friend is for life. They will take unbelievable abuse in a friendship, but if they ever change their minds, which they seldom do, that's it, never will they reconsider that friendship again.

Similarly, they will take a lot of physical abuse. Yet, if backed into a corner, they will use physical force, which may include punching their opponent. This tendency applies to both men and women.

The nature of ones is to leave their homes to pursue new horizons. Children strong in the *one* quality leave home early in life to make their own way and establish their independence. It follows that intimate personal relationships are not their strong point.

PLANT METAPHOR: SEED

How does the nature of a seed compare to the character of a pioneer, the *one* qualities? Seeds are exceptionally strong, independent, durable, and self-sufficient. They are very plain looking and it could be said that they are bald. A seed can remain in its casing for dozens of years — alone, independent, separate from, self-sufficient — and, in a sense, be completely content within itself. Years later, when the seed comes in contact with dirt, water, and warmth from the sun, it will change its form (its mind) and move in a new direction.

Everything that is needed for the oak tree to be an oak tree is contained in the acorn. The seed, the pioneer, is like a diamond in the rough. Only when a diamond is cut and polished can the finished product be appreciated or understood. Notice, therefore, that *ones* don't care if they are understood. They live in their own world, separate from the rest of life.

SENSE METAPHOR: TOUCH

Of the five physical senses, the most dense sense is that of touch. *Ones* are very attuned to physical touch. They don't offer a limp hand shake. In fact, you are well advised to get a solid grip and respond vigorously to avoid a sprained hand. Because *ones* are unbelievably strong, relatively insensitive, people of few words, and primarily attuned to the  physical sense of touch, they often express their affection with a very solid slap on the back. Unfortunately, in their enthusiasm, they can forget their own strength and send the recipient of their affection sailing through the nearest wall.

The physical senses are related to the chakra system. Chakras are energy centers associated with both the physical and etheric bodies of humans. The first seven chakras are located within the physical body beginning with the root chakra at the bottom of the spine. This chakra is related to our sense of security, our survival instincts, and regulates our physical vitality. The pioneer is a superb example of these qualities given his ability to survive in the wilderness with his trusty rifle, single garment of buckskin, and his packet of beef jerky. The true pioneer did not rely on McDonald's for his meal of the day.

The physical vitality of the first chakra is directly linked to sexual vitality. Although *ones* have a strong sexual drive, they are definitely not the type that want to cuddle and chat afterwards. Nor are they much for foreplay. Their style is to get the basic job done, then get on with whatever other practical things need attention — like working on their motor bikes.

ASTROLOGY METAPHOR: ARIES

In the oracle of astrology, each sign of the Zodiac has a natal position in each of the 12 houses. In addition, each sign is ruled by a planet. Although the signs, the planets and the houses each have a different function, their character is similar within their natal positions. For example, Mars rules Aries whose natal position is the first house. The qualities of Mars, Aries and the first house share a common thread.

This common thread also weaves its way through the qualities of the nine numbers in numerology. For the purposes of this book, we will look at the similarities, the common thread, and forgo a comparison of the differences.

Each astrological section builds on the previous one defining an evolutionary pattern of conscious growth beginning with the emergence of the primary ego and building towards full integration of the mature adult. This astrological pattern of growth reflects many similarities and interleaves with the other metaphors used to cultivate an awareness of the qualities of the numbers.

If you have no interest in astrology and its relationship to numerology, simply skip these sections at the conclusion of each of the first 9 chapters. But, if you know even a little bit about astrology, these sections may be helpful as another reference point.

With the above comments in mind, let's look at some of the qualities of Aries which are very similar to the qualities of the *one*.

Aries is natal to the first house of the Zodiac. It is a masculine quality known as a fire sign of action. Aries represents an instinctual, primitive, burst of life-force energy — the basic emergence of the ego. This energy is the uncut diamond, a diamond in the rough, the pioneer. They are their own person with little or no awareness of others. They have a powerful sense of survival.

Aries, like the one, are great initiators. They have the necessary ambition and drive to accomplish what they desire. Aries are the doers. They find their identity in action. If you have something you want done immediately, Aries is the one to do it. But don't try to exert strong leadership on them. They are very independent and refuse to follow anyone who doesn't have true authority. They prefer to do it themselves. They approach life energetically, with a zest and enthusiasm that can be very inspiring to others.

The sign of Aries rules the head, and headstrong they are. Aries have a tendency to dominate, to be quick-tempered and prone to headaches. Like the Ram, which is a symbol for Aries, they charge ahead to get what they want, even if it means confrontation and butting heads with others who stand in their way. They are not known for patience. Aries is the most self-centred and aggressive sign of the Zodiac, forever challenging physical forms and life's boundaries. The key word for Aries is "*I am*". Their focus is on themselves and their attitude is "*You're irrelevant, life is about me*". Although they exude self-confidence on the surface, they often harbour internal feelings of inadequacy. They tend to be instinctual and reactive, with little concern for the outcome or the consequence of their actions.

They are very straightforward, calling it as they see it, and that's that! Honesty is absolute in their minds and diplomacy is an abstraction to them.

Aries love the color red which is the color of action. Red is also the color of the first chakra.

Why Do Numbers Count

CHAPTER 2 — QUALITIES OF THE TWO

Within the four metaphors, the qualities of the TWO are:

PEOPLE	PLANTS	SENSES	ASTROLOGY
WOMAN	SPROUTING	TASTE	TAURUS

PEOPLE METAPHOR: WOMAN

As cited in Chapter 1, the most obvious physical distinction of woman from man is the genitals. The woman's genitals are internal. They are designed to receive and to create within. Whereas, the male is a builder of material, external things; the female is a creator of inner, spiritual qualities. She creates life itself within the womb. The process unfolds in the dark and is shrouded in mystery and magic. Mystically, out of the void, out of the no-thing, emerges the creation and birth of a child — the most miraculous event that we experience on planet earth. It is said that all things are born of the feminine energy.

The male offers external expression to the internal desires of the female. Feminine energy can be likened to an appetite that consumes and absorbs; whereas, the male energy desires to perform and produce for the female. Where the female energy is focused on **being**; the male energy is focused on **doing**. The adage that we are first human beings, not human *doings*, is a direct reflection of the precept that all creation is born of the feminine energy.

The mystical, magical qualities of woman are impossible to figure out using the linear, logical left-brain that is so typically male. Linear and non-linear are mutually exclusive. Unfortunately, men and women spend most of their time spurning the other rather than embracing the differences which are so essential to the fullness of life. Have you ever seen a coin without an opposite side?

And so it is that woman is the polar opposite of man. Where the male is invested in independence, self-sufficiency, and separation, the female energy instinctively seeks to remove boundaries, to fuse, and bond with her environment. Consequently, her natural instinct is not only to give birth to life, it is also to preserve life, and to find resolution for differences that separate.

When secure, she is the natural diplomat and nourishes all life. When insecure, she has no qualms about giving expression to her dark side which knows no boundaries and has no perception of rational. At such times, the shadow figures of her unconscious mind come forward from a realm of unfathomable emotions. In such a state, her wrath is incomprehensible and she can devastate everything in her path. This is an impossible time for the man in her life, who sees her actions and emotions as dramatically disconnected from all reason of the rational mind. His logical, linear, left-brain, style of thinking cannot comprehend the lack of definition and loss of boundaries. He has no context for coping when she is in this state and his survival instinct demands that he detach and leave her to her own resolve. Such action, unfortunately, amplifies the frustration of the polar opposites of man and woman and on goes the battle of who's right. Is left-brain thinking more valid than right-brain? Are boundaries more important than resolving differences that separate? Can we deny the darkness and favour only the light? It strikes me that men and women need to accept each other for who they are and to celebrate their differences. In the final analysis, each of us is a composite of male and female energies.

KEY IMAGE: DIPLOMAT

The qualities of the two are similar to the nature of feminine energy. Twos are naturally right-brained — they are creative, non-linear, and multi-dimensional in their thinking patterns. They can always see both sides of the coin at the same time. Typically, they find themselves in the middle of disputes striving to be the mediator between two of their beloved friends. They hate to say NO to anyone at any time. It hurts them internally to create a boundary by saying no. Consequently, they avoid issues and are masters at telling partial truths and little white lies. It's a challenge for them to be assertive and often they develop a passive-aggressive personality. On the other hand, a two who learns to be assertive and can say no without defence is a natural diplomat and mediator. Notice how opposite the diplomatic personality is from the qualities of the one who couldn't care less what other people think or say or do.

Whatever function or activity a two is pursuing, they always prefer to be with a friend, or better still, with lots of friends. They hate to be alone at any time. They love to shower or bathe with their mate. Sometimes, twos are teased, if not chided, that they can't go to the bathroom without holding someone's hand. Obviously, that's an extreme suggestion, but it does paint an image that isn't readily forgotten.

In contrast to ones who are morning people and love sunrises and being out-of-doors in the sunlight, twos are night people and are comfortable in the dark. They hate to get up in the morning. Even as children, they hate to go to bed in case they will miss something, particularly if there is a party in the home or relatives are visiting. They believe that if God had intended for people to enjoy sunrises, He would have scheduled them later in the day. Twos lack the physical vitality of the one which adds to their slow morning starts. They are only sports-minded to the degree that it offers an opportunity to socialize. Ones are the participants in sports, twos are the spectators.

Where ones are people of few words, twos love to talk about people and relationships. They are masters at "Then he said and she said and he said and she said". Material facts are irrelevant. It's the mood,  the atmosphere, the flavour that is vital. They never approach anything straight on and always beat around the bush — talk in circles. Strangely enough, twos often have a terrible time remembering people's names which is an outrageous embarrassment to them. Never ask a two to keep a secret for more than ten seconds or they may burst at the seams!

In contrast to ones who prefer sturdy, solid furniture, twos love elegant, delicate, refined furniture with lots of frilly detail. They love doilies and teapot cosies. After all, the best part of life for a two is the social atmosphere of a tea party where everyone is nice to everyone else. Camping and the out-of-doors would be bearable in a forty-foot trailer with air conditioning. Although they love luxury, they don't like to work to support their expensive tastes. Shopping is one of their favourite social activities. A two's response to the adage that money can't buy happiness is that such people obviously don't know where to shop.

KEY WORD: EMOTIONS

The female energy is attuned to the emotional content of life which is symbolized by water. Still water runs deep as do the emotions of a two. They cry easily and are deeply impacted by the thoughts and feelings of others. Consequently, they are easily misled in relationships where they tend to live for the other person while sacrificing their own needs. Their love of peace and harmony overrides their discretion and they are perceived to lack discernment and shrewdness. In truth, they are very discerning, however, in their preference to follow rather than lead, they frequently acquiesce to the opinions of others. Twos will spend a lifetime second guessing what others want to hear rather than expressing their own opinions. It's easier for them to let others make the decisions rather than risk any misunderstandings.

The second chakra is approximately two inches above the root chakra. It is the energy of sensual pleasure, sexuality, and the emotions of life. Twos love everything sensual about life. They are natural "cuddlers" and true romantics.

Twos are very sensitive to their environment and surroundings. They excel in creating a "welcome everyone" atmosphere at social gatherings, both in a material sense and as host or hostess.

Water and other fluids are key ingredients in the reproductive process of conception and growth of the fetus. People strong in the two quality readily retain water (edema) and often find it a great struggle to lose weight on a diet. When a two gets a common cold, they will expend a lot of mucus.

Healthwise, they are prone to having weak bladders and weak kidneys. They often slouch in an effort to take the pressure off their kidneys. In keeping with their tendency to lean on others for support and decisions, they lean on door frames and furniture rather than stand alone and be independent.

Because of their attunement to fluids, they love their food moist and covered with sauces. Twos have beautifully smooth skin that is ever so soft. In contrast, their skin can have a rippled appearance such as smooth water ripples when a gust of gentle wind skims its surface.

A major fluid of the body is blood. The gentle, easygoing, lack-of-action nature of twos manifests in poor circulation of their blood. Consequently, they suffer from cold hands and feet. What they consider warm and comfortable is experienced as stuffy and unbearably hot to all the other numbers except sevens and nines.

Twos are like sponges that absorb water quickly and release

what they absorb just as quickly when given a gentle squeeze. Similarly, twos learn very quickly and forget just as fast as they learn. They score very high on exams when they can cram the night before. Twos learn primarily through their emotional experience, whereas ones learn through their physical experience.

PLANT METAPHOR: SPROUTING

Planting a seed in the ground when there is sufficient warmth from the sun is not enough to stimulate the seed to grow. The vital ingredient of water also must be present. A seed only sprouts when it is in an appropriate relationship with its environment. And so it is with the two quality which requires direct contact and appropriate relationships in order to begin to grow in an emotional and personal sense.

Imagine a rock the size of your fist resting on top of a seed which is sprouting. Does the tender sprout attack the rock and strive to push it out of the way, or does the sprout simply acknowledge the rock's presence and grow around it? The sprout is like the two quality that believes that diplomacy and tact are the better part of valour. This attitude is in contrast to the pioneer who directly confronts the environment, material objects, people, and life in general.

The sprouting phase unfolds under the ground and out of sight. Similarly, the value that a two adds to any environment is invisible. Typically, the two is accused of being unproductive and not creating tangible results. They appear to be only socializing and carrying on with endless chitchat of no consequence. Do not be misled! The two is always at work under the surface and is building relationships on feeling and tonal levels which dramatically impacts the quality of relationships. They are natural diplomats and do exceptionally well as public relations workers, foreign diplomats, mediators, psychologists, and in sales positions that require a gentle touch and a soft sell.

SENSE METAPHOR: TASTE

Because twos are attuned to fluids, their sense of taste is very keen.

Infants and children initially explore their environment by touching and tasting. First they touch objects, then bang them, and, if at all possible, put the object into their mouth. Dirt, rocks, paper, toys, it doesn't matter — first touch, then taste.

Twos love to eat because they love to taste!! Given their inactive nature and tendency to retain fluids, twos gain weight easily. They have to take extreme measures to lose weight on a diet.

ASTROLOGY METAPHOR: TAURUS

Taurus is ruled by Venus, Goddess of Love, and is natal to the second house of the Zodiac. Many qualities of Taurus are feminine in nature and reflect an awareness of duality and other people. In essence, they are very different from Aries who are fundamentally only aware of themselves.

Taurus is deeply bonded to their surroundings. Their deep sense of oneness with all things is only possible because they do not hold themselves separate from their environment. Unlike

Aries who spends a lifetime defining boundaries and challenging them, Taurus dislikes boundaries between themselves and the rest of life. Ask a Taurus to change their mind once they have set a boundary and you will be faced with a very rigid, stubborn attitude that is unwilling to change.

Taurus has a love of harmony and will be very diplomatic in order to maintain peace. They are very proficient at creating an atmosphere where love can be shared. There is a healing quality to Taurus. In their presence, we feel a sense of calm, not to worry, all is well, and everything will be fine forever. Because Taurus is ruled by Venus, it is their nature to remember all the emotional detail.

They enjoy physical comfort and ease. They have a love of physical pleasures and can be very demonstrative of their affection. They love beauty, good books, music, and art where there is a sense of harmony and a gentle interplay of opposing qualities.

Their love of ease can create an inertia which takes some doing to overcome. Once started, however, Taurus has the patience, persistence, and perseverance to stay with a project through to completion. They derive great satisfaction from being constructive and cultivating lasting and worthwhile creations, including both material objects and relationships with family and friends. But the pace is slow and deliberate. The gift of Taurus is that they provide security, stability, and loyalty. They feel best about themselves when they feel they have given birth to something tangible.

Taurus people experience themselves as very slow learners and often harbour a deep concern that God forgot some vital parts of their brain. This experience comes from their unwillingness to change and to set boundaries, which is the nature of the feminine, Taurus energy of being that contrasts the masculine,

Aries energy of doing.

They have a deep longing for authenticity. They cannot pretend that they are having fun if they are not. Nor can they rush a job just to get it done. It's very difficult for a Taurus to comprehend how anyone can do things quickly and actually enjoy themselves.

The keynote phrase for Taurus is "I have". They must be financially secure before they will rest well at night.

Similar to the seed that sprouts under the ground where it is out of sight, Taurus people are very shy and don't like to be watched. They love to grow gardens and house plants which reflects their sense of oneness with nature.

Like the two quality, Taureans adore creamy things, such as ice cream and chocolate.

A SUMMARY OF THE NUMBERS 1 & 2

The **I CHING**, the Chinese **Book of Changes**, speaks of a basic polarity of all life which at one end is Yang energy and at the other end Yin. Similarly, the numbers 1 & 2 symbolize the polar opposites of human nature. It's valuable to formulate a clear perspective of the polarities as all the remaining qualities complete the spectrum between the extremities.

The following table compares the difference between Yang and Yin which correspond to the qualities of the numbers 1 and 2.

YANG (ONE)	YIN (TWO)
time	space
individualization	relationship
hierarchy	community
polarity	unity
judging	forgiveness
purpose, doing	existence, being
utilize	nourish
external form	Internal spirit
discriminating	accepting
differences	similarities, resemblances
dividing, separating	embracing, resolve
organize, initiate	yield, receive
leads	follows
planned	spontaneous
rigid	flexible
arrogance	devotion
identify, label	feel, blend, harmonize
manifest	conceptualize
create	allow
dictate	listen, reflect
sceptical	trusting
focus, specialize	generalize
cool, isolated	warm, open
demanding	gentle, accommodating
aggressive, active	passive, reserved, peaceful

YANG (ONE)

fission, separate
fragmented
detached
understanding
light
death

YIN (TWO)

fusion, bonded, oneness
integrated
compassionate
wisdom
dark
birth

Although these conceptual differences can manifest as polar opposites in men and women, they are more commonly perceived to exist in a blended format as depicted by the symbol of Yin/Yang.

In the Yin/Yang symbol the differences are represented by a light side and a dark side separated by a curved line that fades gently into the opposites. In further

acknowledgement that the differences are fluid and not fixed, there exists two smaller circles of opposite tones within the opposing halves. The Yin/Yang circle is very different from a rigid box with a straight line sharply dividing the box into equal halves. I doubt that life fits into such ridged, fixed boxes. Even so, the perception of polar opposites is a valuable starting point for defining the vast spectrum of human qualities.

CHAPTER 3 — QUALITIES OF THE THREE

Within the four metaphors, the qualities of the THREE are:

PEOPLE	PLANTS	SENSES	ASTROLOGY
CHILD	FIRST LEAF	SMELL	GEMINI

PEOPLE METAPHOR: CHILD

When the polar opposites of man and woman bond, a child is born. A child is a composite of the best of both worlds of the numbers one and two. It's the balance point of the two opposites.

Children are like the one in that they have unbelievable strength and endurance. They are independent, demanding, and embarrassingly truthful. Unless abused, they do not question their survival.

Children are like the two in that they are innocent, loving, and very sociable. They laugh easily, cry easily, and forget hurts quickly as long as they are shown understanding and appreciation. They love to talk and, too often, it absolutely doesn't matter what they are talking about as long as they can make a lot of noise. Children will do almost everything to excess unless they learn how to set boundaries.

Children are inquisitive, they love to learn, and are not afraid of making mistakes. When learning how to walk, they will fall down a thousand times a day and all the time they laugh. Life is a game to be enjoyed. Better still, it's all a fantasy and it's silly to take any of it seriously. Threes, like children, love to tease and argue simply to see what happens next. If you say it's a sunny day, they will say it's a cloudy day just to get something going. If you get a little mad at their game, so much the better because, in their mind, any drama makes life more exciting and less predictable. At a party, threes will entice two people into a discussion with the intention of creating a debate and hopefully an argument. Once they get the ball rolling, they enjoy sitting back and watching the sparks fly. It's the feelings of the drama that they love, although they don't enjoy the game if it gets too serious.

Threes are party animals and inhale junk food. They adore sweets because of the high energy it gives them. Excessive sugar adds to their tendency to swing from one extreme to the other. Like children, threes are blessed with good luck, and at the eleventh hour, Lady Luck always saves the day. When a three is in the depths of despair, tell them the latest joke, no matter how silly it may be, and they will bounce back to life immediately, forgetting that they had decided life was over. They have a wonderful sense of humour and an exceptionally deep, loud laugh.

Children live in a fantasy world where they pretend to take things seriously, but in reality they see life as a game. Their vivid imaginations can run wild and completely exclude concrete reality. Consequently, arithmetic is difficult for them. Their fantasy-filled, unstructured world has little or no concept of time. Hence, both as children and as adults, they are seldom, if ever, on time for appointments.

KEY IMAGE: ENTERTAINER, EXTROVERT

Threes are spontaneous, dynamic entertainers and extroverted by nature. They love to show off. Their gift for playing music and singing, combined with their wonderful sense of humour and ability to talk, creates an outstanding presence on stage. They thrive on acknowledgement and excitement — the more dramatic, the better. Consequently, as children, they don't walk straight, they skip and twirl wherever they go.

Similarly, their handwriting is full of curlicues and scrolls, and they always draw circles when they doodle.

Children are full of the spirit of life, they are inspired and inspirational by nature. Threes find it easy to inspire others with their enthusiasm. Inspiration goes hand-in-hand with being creative, spiritual, and forgiving. Threes can be truly magnetic. They are much more positive in opinion than they are in action.

Children are the hope for our future. Their innocence and trust inspire a promise of a more humane tomorrow. With the ups and downs of life, it's important to embrace the essence of the three quality — to maintain a sense of humour, not to fear falling down when we are learning, and always to be willing to stand up and try again no matter how many times we fail. Threes instinctively know that life works. To them, life is simply a big game of "Clue" and is designed first and foremost to be fun and full of surprises. Although children are inquisitive about everything possible, they get bored easily and quickly lose their concentration. Similarly, threes truly love discovering and experiencing the zest of living, although they are quick to move from one experience to the next.

Healthwise, because threes are extroverts, they are subject to skin rashes. As teenagers, they particularly suffer from acne because they indulge in sweets and junk food.

PLANT METAPHOR: FIRST LEAF

Imagine building a new home and spending endless weeks doing the landscaping yourself. The lawn has been planted and it's been a war with the neighbourhood kids and dogs to keep them off your future lawn. Endless days go by and no grass appears — just your luck, you bought a bag of dead grass seed. And then, just when you finally gave up, there it is, little green sprouts of grass everywhere. You are ecstatic and run into the house to tell your spouse that it is actually happening. You find her upstairs and take her to the window to show her that miracles are real. From the second floor of your home, not one new blade is visible and she tells you that you have had too much sun — you need a rest she says. More than a little concerned that she may be right, you persevere and insist that she go outside to see for herself. Arriving outdoors, you are greatly relieved and rebound to your state of ecstasy that the seeds had in fact grown as they were supposed to grow. Your spouse responds with a shrug and asks what did you expect.

That's the nature of the threes experience. Excitable, running up to the second floor, making a great fuss about the obvious, down the stairs in doubt and great disappointment, only to bounce back to the exuberant amazement that life works.

Threes swing from one extreme to the other, generally landing back on their feet after any major upset.

SENSE METAPHOR: SMELL

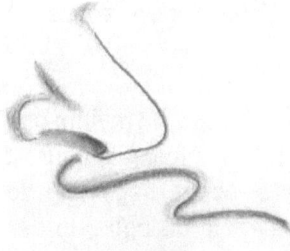

The five physical senses of touch, taste, smell, hearing, and sight can be compared on the basis of the density or the frequency at which they operate. The sense of touch is in response to physical objects. The sense of taste is in response to physical objects which are being broken down into liquids and becoming less dense. When liquids are heated and begin to vaporize, they stimulate our olfactory bulbs and create the sense of smell.

Threes are attuned to the sense of smell. As dinner guests or as a spouse arriving home for dinner, the first thing they will do is lift the lid of each pot and smell what is cooking, then they will pursue the other more conventional social graces, such as asking if you had a nice day.

The third chakra resides in the area of the solar plexus and is known as the seat of power, self-will and determination. Threes embrace these qualities with gusto.

ASTROLOGICAL METAPHOR: GEMINI

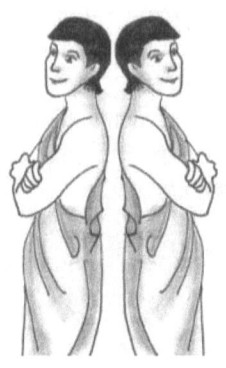

Gemini is natal to the third house of the Zodiac and represents the beginning of the mind's cognitive process.

Before we identify Gemini, let's summarize the nature of the first two signs. Aries is a burst of raw, instinctual, masculine energy that is essentially only aware of itself. Aries explores the boundaries of life through action. Taurus becomes aware of duality, other people, and of the emotional currents of life. They want to understand the nature of others while holding their own rhythm and their own sense of beingness.

Gemini begins to ask just how do we stay in our own rhythm and our own beingness. They begin the process of trying to figure it all out. The three and Gemini are about beginning to conceptually discover the nature of reality, to dialogue, to ask questions, to read, to write, to begin to piece the puzzle together.

Gemini rebounds out of the Taurean's kinaesthetic state of being and steadfast single-mindedness. Now we are in Gemini who can't remember for a moment how to be steadfast. They want to change all the options, change their minds in a split second, go into their heads, and begin to intellectually understand as compared to kinaesthetically feel. This is a phase of pursuing knowledge, understanding, and information.

Gemini has a capacity to be like a child in their hunger and quest for versatility and being able to tickle itself into interesting topics.

Gemini becomes bored very quickly unless there is mental stimulation or there is something new to be discovered. At their worst, Gemini's can be gossipers and exaggerators and will challenge frivolous issues simply to pass the time of day. Gemini has a tendency to fall victim to superficiality simply to keep itself interested in the game of life. As a consequence, they will indulge in drama and playfulness that isn't really authentic. They can intellectually gnaw away at analysis and criticism. The challenge of the three and Gemini is to learn how to focus their intellectual ability.

The greatest gift of Gemini is their sincere interest to understand life. At their vulnerable point, Gemini becomes critical and analytical and forgets to keep their heart present within the analytical process. When a Gemini's heart and mind are aligned, they can be quite brilliant in their capacity to articulate the world around them. If Geminis exclusively use their intellectual prowess to move through their world, their approach tends to be cold hearted and scientific when interacting with family, friends, and business.

They are curious about everything and love to explore life and gather information simply for information's sake. Their attention span is short and their intellect can be somewhat childlike and basic, although their memories are excellent. They have little or no sense of direction in life. Gemini's are playful, elusive, and hard to pin down. They have superb verbal skills and it's hard to tell if their stories are fact or fantasy. One of their great fears is being caught embellishing fact with fiction. As long as the topic of conversation keeps changing, they never get bored with small talk, and are in their element at social functions.

CHAPTER 4 — QUALITIES OF THE FOUR

Within the four metaphors, the qualities of the FOUR are:

PEOPLE	PLANTS	SENSES	ASTROLOGY
STUDENT	ROOTS	HEARING	CANCER

PEOPLE METAPHOR: STUDENT

Once children have had 4 or 5 years to develop physically, they begin their formal education by going to school. Historically, schools have focused on linear, logical, detailed, rote learning. It was imperative that the student show all the details of their long division!! Not much emphasis, if any, was given to the creative, conceptual, artistic side of human nature.

The four quality represents everything that the old school system did. They are serious, determined, well-disciplined people. They keep their appointments to the minute, with a seriousness similar to getting to the next class at school and being in one's seat before the bell stops ringing. A four will say, "When I say that I'll meet you at one o'clock, I mean one o'clock, not two minutes before or two minutes after. Do you understand?"

KEY IMAGE: ANALYZER

Fours are the ultimate analyzers always in need of more data before they can make a decision. They are obsessed with figuring everything out. As children, they will spend days taking old clocks apart to see how they work. They want to know why. They embrace the classic attitude of "I'm from Missouri. Don't tell me, show me!" If someone gives them verbal directions on how to find a specific location, they won't even listen to the directions. They will write down the address, agree to everything that is said, and after the conversation, they will get out a map, look up the location, and decide for themselves how they will travel to the place in question.

As the ultimate analyzers, they lead a very fixed and scheduled life. They hate surprises and in fact become upset and disoriented when their schedule is not followed to the letter. Certainly they are very opposite in this regard to the three who thrives on surprises and change. Because fours dislike change, they don't like holidays unless they can stay at home and do repairs on the house and yard. Their preference for no change reflects in their appreciation for history, tradition, ceremony, and rituals, although they are not spiritually or romantically inclined.

The fours idea of doodling is to draw straight lines, squares, and cubes. They print precisely on the lines of ruled paper. If their writing paper is not ruled, they will print along the edge of the ruler to keep their printing straight. Even knives and forks on a table must be aligned correctly. A crooked picture on a wall is enough to drive a four crazy. They simply can't sit still in a room with a crooked picture until they walk over and straighten it. They are immaculate housekeepers. If they have a workshop, the tools will each have their own peg on the wall with an outline of the tool that goes on that peg. Everything must be in its proper place. I doubt that a four has ever walked into a room, home or office, when they haven't scanned the layout to determine if it was organized in the most efficient manner possible. Their eye for balance, efficiency, detail, and spatial relationships allows them to be excellent interior designers and architects.

Fours take a long time to digest any new idea or concept. When it comes to food, their slow digestion results in constipation. Fours typically gain weight around the abdomen, buttocks, and thighs. Their lack of flexibility reflects in their unique style of walking with a rigid upper body that sways from side to side.

The four quality is the first truly intellectual quality in the number sequence of 1 to 9. Fours want to know the truth down to the finest detail. Their inquisitiveness and attention to detail make them natural builders.  Their patience and tenacity also serve them well in completing what they start. As a consequence, they can accumulate a respectable, if not significant, financial base over a lifetime. Even so, it should be emphasized that their accumulation is based on a lot of old-fashioned, hard work and penny-pinching.

A four will often spend many hours completing a project which is no longer required simply because they only begin what they intend to complete. Most people consider such efforts to be impractical, if not meaningless. Undoubtedly, only the fours reading this book will know exactly what I mean about the deep, soothing sense of satisfaction that comes from completing a project that was not compromised. It's as if the project itself has a life and a birthright to experience completion.

Too often, the four quality is belittled. Yet, without the organizational skill of the four, life itself would be chaos and confusion. The four quality is a vital ingredient in the cake mix. They constantly ask, "What is truly going on here? How does it work? How can I make it work more efficiently?" These are important questions for anyone desiring to improve their life.

Isn't life a delightful paradox? The four who appears to despise change on one hand, constantly seeks to improve and make changes on the other.

PLANT METAPHOR: ROOTS

Once a seed sprouts and generates its first leaf, the newborn plant has a very specific challenge to meet.

Have you ever noticed how the daffodils poke their noses out of the ground in the spring and then seem to just sit there for a week or ten days and not grow? At this point, all the nourishment of the bulb has been spent, and the plant must develop its root system to become self-sustaining before the next step of growth can take place. This is a very vulnerable time for the plant because so many things can go wrong at this stage. The growth will terminate if the climate is too hot or too

cold, too wet or too dry, if the cow eats it, or steps on it.
Root systems branch out to become very, very fine in order to absorb the mineral traces in the soil and to capture water. They are exceptionally detailed in design just as the four is exceptionally detailed by nature. The purpose of the root system is to allow the plant to stand on its own "two feet" and be self-sufficient.

A root system is underground. Under the ground is symbolic of the subconscious mind which goes deeper than the conscious mind. People strong in the fours are always looking deeper, for the underlying principles involved. They don't take life superficially. Rather, they see life as very complex — something to be constantly analyzed.

SENSE METAPHOR: HEARING

In the progression of touch, taste, and smell, the next least dense sense is hearing. Either fours have perfect pitch or they have a tin ear.

There are always two sides to a coin — whatever exists on one side of the coin, the opposite lives on the other side. As in the example at hand, a four in their natural state will hear with perfect pitch or they will have made a conscious choice to ignore their natural gift and will swing the pendulum to the opposite extreme. This is a good point to remember about the qualities of the numbers from 1 to 9 — each number has both positive and negative qualities and each person chooses which quality to embrace from moment to moment.

The fourth chakra is related to the heart. One who can hear the way of the heart in meticulous detail and can follow their heart is a gifted and blessed person. Fours who choose to listen to their heart are marvellous healers who leave nothing to chance. Their inspiration is always well grounded in practicality.

ASTROLOGICAL METAPHOR: CANCER

Cancer is natal to the fourth house of the Zodiac. Within every Cancer is the emotional depth of Taurus and the inquisitive mind of Gemini. Cancer wants to take the cognitive process of Gemini a step deeper and to truly understand the feelings of Taurus.

The nature of Cancer is similar to the four who puts roots deep into the earth so they can absorb all the nutrients required to nourish themselves and their family. Cancers love to cook, to nourish, to build homes, and be the caretakers of their family and friends.

The root system, which penetrates deep into the earth, symbolizes delving into the subconscious mind. In this sense, fours and Cancer are deeply in touch with the emotional currents of life and bring to the surface (into awareness) subconscious beliefs and feelings. As they become aware of these deep currents, they set out to analyze what is happening in their personal world. It is common for Cancer and the four to become lost in analyzing their environment and everyone else's feelings to the point where they lose touch with their own. This tendency leaves Cancer in the shadows of many substantial misunderstandings — how do we resolve the dilemma of an extremely emotional person who is stuck in analysis and out of touch with themselves?

Cancer tends to be one of the most misinterpreted signs of the

Zodiac, as is four in numerology. Another basis of their confusion lies in the fact that society doesn't understand the function of the subconscious mind and fears any aspect of deep feelings — especially feelings like sadness or depression. In their lack of understanding, people interpret Cancer to be a victim consciousness and are unable to appreciate the true depth of Cancer's feelings.

It is common for Cancer to misinterpret their sensitivity as cause to be self-conscious, embarrassed, and feeling inadequate. The truth is they have a huge capacity for feelings and offer the gift of compassion and a real sense of caring and love. They are such outstanding caretakers precisely because they are so finely in tune with the feelings and needs of others.

The challenge for Cancer is to establish strong boundaries. They need a steady foundation that they call home where they know their nest. Within their home, they can regroup and find their stability. From a stable home environment, they can be most effective in both business and family matters. In fact, Cancer and Capricorn have more business acumen than any other astrological sign. When Cancer is feeling safe, their analytical and organizational skills come to the fore and they are master builders of structures — especially ones that benefit the wellbeing of family, friends, and community.

If their home front is not secure, safe, and balanced, they become endless worriers who withhold their feelings and dread having their personal secrets told. One of their greatest challenges is letting go of emotions and personal items — they hold onto and save everything just like the four. Consequently, they take solace in history and the way it used to be.

Cancer rules the stomach. When they are under stress, they don't digest their food properly and suffer from gastro-intestinal disorders.

CHAPTER 5 — QUALITIES OF THE FIVE

Within the four metaphors, the qualities of the FIVE are:

PEOPLE	PLANTS	SENSES	ASTROLOGY
TRAVELLER	RAPID GROWTH	SIGHT	LEO

PEOPLE METAPHOR: TRAVELLER

Once people complete their education, they have a great desire to travel and see the world for themselves. They demand freedom and thrive on the change that travel brings. It's a refreshing relief from the classroom where they were forced to conform and regurgitate what the system wanted to hear. The five has had it with conforming and enjoys any opportunity to rebel and to expose the truth.

Where the four dislikes change and making quick decisions, the five thrives on change. They constantly put themselves in challenging positions where they can live on the edge and pit themselves against danger. For a five to come face to face with death is thrilling and they love the total sense of aliveness that such experiences give them. Consequently, they ski fast, drive fast, walk fast. They are intense and very quick minded.

The qualities of the five can be likened to that of young adulthood which is a developmental phase that bridges the gap between the adolescent and the true adult. (For sake of discussion, childhood can be defined from birth to 9, adolescence from 10 to 18, and young adult from 19 to 27.) During childhood and adolescence, we can't wait to complete school and get a job. Often we are intent on showing Mom and Dad how it should be done. Our actions stem more from revenge and arrogance than from maturity and responsibility. Underlying the bravado is a sense of insecurity and doubt. If only we make enough noise, possibly no one will notice our lack of self-esteem.

Fives have a great deal of confidence and ability, yet their confidence has not matured and they are impulsive and impatient. Although it appears they want to reinvent the world and discard everything old, their true desire is to transform the world into a sane place to live. They are somewhat naive and idealistic in their vision which leads to misunderstandings and many bitter, personal experiences. These people have all the vitality and determination of people in their twenties.

KEY IMAGE: PROMOTER

Their discerning eye and exceptionally quick mind are constantly on the lookout for new insights, new ideas, new inventions, new systems, etc. Once they discover something new, they vigorously promote that everyone use their new product or embrace their new idea. Strength of conviction, sharp intellect, and enthusiasm are convincing tools that fives use superbly well.

Analytically, they are like the fours that want all the facts and want to know exactly what the truth of the matter is. Unlike the four, however, the five does not hold out for one more piece of data. Once they sense that all the facts are in, they make a definitive decision and then stick to their guns no matter what. In other words, once fives give their word, they will never go back on it. For example, if a marriage is utterly unworkable and holds the potential for disastrous results, the five will not renege on their wedding vows. Their word is their honour. Fives go through great turmoil when someone doesn't keep an agreement with them. They simply cannot fathom how people can break their word.

Fives have very, very strong likes and dislikes for people, places, events, and things. Combined with their very strong intuitive sense and their demanding nature for the truth, it's an

intense and fiery experience to be around a five. No stone is left unturned, resulting in transformation or destruction. Their hunches hit them in their solar plexus and can cause a "nervous stomach". When they get backed into a corner, the tension builds in their solar plexus like a turn-key. Either they release the tension constructively or they explode into a caustic and contemptuous harangue. They can be very cruel. As soon as their outburst is over, they will have deep regrets for their bitter expression and spend days crucifying themselves for their actions. After they emerge from a period of deep depression, they will exercise extreme discipline to prevent further explosions. Although their willpower and discipline are exceptional, and to be admired, discipline can only keep the lid on internal discontent for so long before physical limits are reached. At such times, their intense optimism gives way to pessimism, depression and thoughts of suicide. This process can be a difficult catch-22 until fives learn ways to constructively direct or release their intense energies.

Their knife-edge, hair-trigger character manifests in a chiselled appearance with small, tight lines around their mouth and eyes. They tend to walk with their head and body leaning forward and with their chin out in defiance of life. They find it virtually impossible to relax and will go until exhausted, often running on nervous energy alone. Typically, they are lean regardless of how much they eat.

When fives meet someone new, it only takes them a fraction of a second to completely make up their mind about the person. They tend to berate themselves for their immediate judgement of people and strive diligently to remain open and give people a chance to prove themselves. Without fail, their first impression proves to be valid. After the fact, they crucify themselves endlessly for going against their own knowing. Fives need to learn to trust and respect their intuition and not to see their likes and dislikes as judgements. Their intuition and discernment is intended to assist them in finding personal freedom and living their own truth, free from tradition, ceremony, and the collective consciousness.

Fives will try their hand at anything and everything. If they decide to learn to play a guitar, they will practice morning, noon, and night. Within a few months they will be playing complex music with great skill. Then, as quickly as the impulse came, it will leave and the guitar will be put in a closet, never to be played again.

PLANT METAPHOR: RAPID GROWTH

Once the plant has developed its root system, a period of rapid growth takes place. As quickly as the stock grows, branches spring out in all directions. The rapid growth cannot happen unless the root system is well developed and can access the necessary raw materials. In addition, the expansiveness of the root system dictates how much support will be given to the height of the plant. It doesn't serve the plant to outgrow its foundation such that it falls over and dies. Hence, the analytical foundation of the four dictates how much the five can branch out and interact in all arenas of life.

SENSE METAPHOR: SIGHT

Following touch, taste, smell, and hearing, is sight, which operates on the highest frequency range of the 5 physical senses. Fives have a very critical eye. As children, they don't care how their food tastes or smells. If it doesn't look right, there is no way that they will eat it.

The fifth chakra is located in the throat and is associated with the thyroid gland. This chakra is attributed the qualities of creativity, vision, and telepathy which are common to the five.

Their critical, discerning eye is most insightful and often finds an artistic outlet drawing caricature cartoons. They are very quick to give accurate and direct advice, but their fierce independence bitterly resents being given any advice in return. Fives are notorious for remembering insults and will spend years dreaming of revenge.

ASTROLOGY METAPHOR: LEO

Leo is natal to the fifth house of the Zodiac and represents creative self-expression and the development of a rich, full personality.

Where Aries is a burst of raw, instinctual energy, and is essentially only aware of itself, Taurus became aware of the differences between itself and others. Next, Gemini begins to ask questions about the differences and Cancer became concerned with caring for others, understanding their feelings and to establish a secure home base from which to operate. The next step of evolution brings Leo who wants to express its will, to put itself out into the world with full colour, uninhibited, and unabashed. As contradictory as it may seem, Leo has a deep need for acceptance and a fear of rejection. Within their heart, their concern is "Will you like me? Are you going to applaud when I finish? Are you going to reject me?"

Leo reaches outside of itself to establish an identity, an outer-persona, and to complete the development of the ego that Aries began. This is an important stage of individuating into physical reality and Leo should be acknowledged for their willingness to reach beyond the confines and safety of home. They should be applauded for their willingness to risk and to develop a dynamic personality. In this vulnerable posture of venturing beyond the security of home, Leo is like the adolescent or the young adult who is uncertain in this new territory and are looking for validation for their actions and their personhood. They are truly courageous like their sign, the Lion, yet, they harbour a fear of rejection.

Leo's pleasure and joy comes from expressing their ego. Through their vitality, joy, entertainment, and excitement of being alive, Leo inspires us to action. Where Cancer felt everyone's feelings to the point of feeling victimized, Leo takes control and expresses their will refusing to let anyone else control their emotions. In fact, Leo, will control your emotions by inspiring you, by making you laugh, by making you cry, by being the actress or the actor.

Leos have a huge capacity to change, be creative, versatile, and lend themselves to being publicly embarrassed. Because we all see and hear Leo, there appears to be no shyness here. They present a persona that seems very self-confident, courageous, and ambitious. Behind the mask of the actor and actress is the vulnerability of Cancer. Although Leo appears very self-confident, they harbour a great sense of inferiority and insecurity. They fear that others may not like them for who they are. Leo can be the actor and not always tell the truth about what they are feeling. Leo embraces the adolescent quality of feeling invincible and no one is big enough to stop them. They have all the answers and an absolute arrogance that propels them into motion only to be stopped by reality. Inherent in Leo and the five is an insecurity that people will ultimately reject them upon really discovering who they perceive themselves to be. Their presentation of who they seem to be and who they really are don't match — their persona is incomplete, it's still growing.

Leo rules the heart, the sense of connectedness of love given and received. Their awareness of love is childlike, idealistic, naive, and very trusting. They are like the innocent adolescent who falls in love for the first time, intoxicated with loving and everything wonderful. It comes as a great surprise when their utopia is inevitably shattered by the reality of everyday living.

Leos are creative, enthusiastic, vibrant, animated, and very alive. They can be dramatic, flamboyant, and sometimes very bossy. Like Aries, they exude an ambience of being the center of the universe. Leo is the story of the Lion who is a kitty cat, licking its wounds and harbouring a real sense of futility and dismay because they believe no one really loves them and it's all been for not. Once they learn to be their own person, to validate themselves, they become dependable, loyal, and very happy.

Fives and Leos are compelled to being creative in how they dress, in how they communicate, and in how they do everything. They have a sense of flair and a sense of real style. Their self-expression is uninhibited, very unique, and openly presented for everyone to see.

CHAPTER 6 — QUALITIES OF THE SIX

Within the four metaphors, the qualities of the SIX are:

PEOPLE	PLANTS	SENSES	ASTROLOGY
FAMILY	BUDDING	MIND	VIRGO

PEOPLE METAPHOR: FAMILY

Once children have completed their formal education and have seen the world, their attention turns to creating a home and a family. To purchase a home and begin a family requires that people be mature, accountable, responsible, and sensible.

The six represents the true adult stage of growth following the developmental phase of the young adult, the five, who has grown beyond adolescence, yet lacks the maturity of experience. Experience is a powerful teacher and affords an internal sixth sense of knowing. The six, with their deep sense of knowingness, is not motivated to promote wholesale change like the five does.

The six has an *interdependent*, family nature which embraces a quality of practical wisdom. They exude harmony, balance, stability, and a congenial, wholesome nature. They are self-assured and draw from their own inner resources creating a continuous string of quiet successes.

Sixes have a predisposed desire to marry early in life and start a family. Serving their family is a way of life and comes naturally to them. Anyone who visits the home of a six is made to feel like one of the family.

The paternal and maternal instincts of the six extend beyond the family and into the community but not into the level of professional politics.

As a rule of thumb, the odd numbers (1-3-5-7-9) are inspirational by nature, whereas the even numbers (2-4-6-8) are practical. The six is unique in this context. The ability to compute a six by multiplying either 2 x 3 or 3 x 2 suggests that the six is any combination of inspirational and practical qualities. On one hand, the six is creative, artistic, musical and inspirational, and, on the other, it is practical, sensible, logical, reasonable and accountable. Sixes embrace the best of both worlds and are capable of graciously accomplishing virtually anything that they desire.

Whereas the knife-edge of the impetuous five is always striving to break free of the confines of tradition and rootedness that the four thrives on, the six has overcome the boundaries of physical reality and is operating from an integrated sense of knowing.

The six doesn't have the impulsive urge for change and travel that the five does. They are relatively content with the status quo and are similar to the four who resists change and new adventures.

Their basic weakness is assuming too much responsibility for both themselves and others. They can be very nosy and are quick to point out the way it "should be" in their well informed opinion. Consequently, they can worry too much and are susceptible to developing migraine headaches. Otherwise, they are well-balanced and capable people.

As you come to know the six quality, the word <u>sensible</u> becomes progressively more appropriate for capturing their essence. The "sensible six" is always busy being a parent to everyone who comes their way.

PLANT METAPHOR: BUDDING

After the plant has developed a root system, grown a stock, and branched out in all directions, the procreative process begins. For the plant this is the budding season prior to the blossom time. Women strong in the sixes are  very fertile and often conceive more readily than they would prefer. Both men and women strong in the six quality have a strong desire for home and family.

SENSE METAPHOR: MIND

After the five physical senses of touch, taste, smell, hearing, and sight, comes the sixth sense of mind which functions on a frequency base higher than the five physical senses. The sixth sense is synonymous with the third eye, the sixth chakra which is one's inner sense of vision.

Have you ever asked someone how they knew what they just said, and they responded, "I don't know, just my sixth sense, I guess."?

The sixth sense is mind, knowing, intuition. People strong in the six quality are extremely intelligent. For them, learning is primarily a process of being reminded of what they already know. They are so used to being "tuned in", no matter what the topic is, that they habitually nod at whatever is said and repeatedly say, "I know ... I know". Their "I know" attitude can drive their friends and co-workers to distraction. Sometimes when a friend gets angry enough, they will vigorously challenge the six and point out there was absolutely no way that they could have possibly known what was being presented. Even when the six may admit that they didn't know, inside their head they have their doubts and will maintain that they, in fact, did know.

Even though the six tends to live in a deja vu world, they have an air of being sensible and accountable in their perceptions. Although it rarely comes to pass, a six can be so enmeshed by their knowingness that they get confused about reality and can become insane. For a six to reach a state of insanity, radical, extenuating, external forces of conditioning were imposed during childhood.

ASTROLOGY METAPHOR: VIRGO

Virgo is native to the sixth house of the Zodiac. Where Gemini represents the beginning of the cognitive process, Virgo takes the mental process to the next level of evolution.

They strive to synthesize and process the data explored by Gemini and collected by Cancer. Virgo seeks to find the value and the purpose of life. They have an inherent wisdom and an ability to assimilate life's experiences. They recognize that the body is a messenger of the unconscious. This recognition, combined with their sense of service, directs them to focus in the medical profession where they work with healing of the physical body. They also make good doctors, nurses, and teachers because they instinctively ask "What's wrong?" and have a knowing of how to fix any problem.

For Leo, life is a playground, whereas for Virgo, life is about developing skills and applying creativity to specific goals. Their inherent wisdom and knowingness sees how life could be. As a result, their favourite word is "should" — you should do this, you should do that, it should be this way or that. Virgo is known as the most critical sign of the Zodiac. They long to organize and simplify physical form to reflect the purity of life's spirit. And when things don't occur as they would like, there is criticism. The challenge for everyone else is to accept their criticism and understand that Virgo's intent is not to hurt but simply to share advice and wisdom.

They don't forget anything and only talk if there is a purpose to talking. They must have something to do, something to be responsible for. Their interests extend beyond home and family into the community at large.

Where Cancer is the caretaker and loves to mother everyone, Virgo's posture is more likened to the mature adult and the parent. It could be said that Virgo fosters the children, Cancer looks after them, and Leo takes them on field trips to explore their world beyond the confines of home. In this sense, Cancer, Leo, and Virgo cultivate and educate the children like the numbers four, five, and six which are also about cultivation.

The first six houses of astrology represent the development of the lower hemisphere of physical life, including the development of the primary ego, establishment of a sense of self, and a connection to nature. The upper hemisphere represents the more ethereal, refined, and spiritual unfoldment of life and the ability to truly interact and relate to others.

CHAPTER 7 — QUALITIES OF THE SEVEN

Within the four metaphors, the qualities of the SEVEN are:

PEOPLE	PLANTS	SENSES	ASTROLOGY
PHILOSOPHER	BLOSSOM	SPIRIT	LIBRA

PEOPLE METAPHOR: PHILOSOPHER

The previous chapter discussed the sixth stage of growth as creating a home for the purpose of having a family. The next step is the birth of the child and the dramatic changes that occur as a result. Suddenly, life is much more than meets the physical eye. In your arms is an infant that was born with a personality, a spirit all of its own. Life takes on a new meaning and a whole new dimension as the reality of the spiritual essence of life sinks into one's consciousness. This is the seventh stage which demands we philosophically come to grips with life.

At first, this stage is overwhelming, confusing, and disorienting. Life isn't what we thought it was. It's so very much more. A million questions spring to mind and one is full of awe and wonder. It's a very precious, tender, magical, mystical time of awakening to a new dimension of reality. We can be overcome with a strong sense of being blessed and honoured to participate in the creation of life. The sense of wonder leaves us lost for words — possibly, there are no words to capture the experience of birth and holding a newborn in our arms.

The seven quality is that of the philosopher and the poet. The words of accomplished orators, philosophers, and poets are not as important as the spaces between the words and the meaning between the lines that capture the heart of their message.

The musician does the same with music. The notes are important, but the timing and the spaces between the notes create depth, texture, and the true magic. Music permeates the very marrow of a seven's bones. Music is divine to them and a magical place of refuge.

Loud, discordant noise upsets their nervous system and is painful to their body.

The depth and uniqueness of feelings that a seven experiences render words inept to capture the essence of their experience. They express themselves better at writing than they do verbally, although they are superb actors because their presence speaks louder than their words. On the stage, the seven can access and express the deepest emotions. In contrast to their outstanding ability to be intimate with an audience, one-on-one, personal relationships are a great struggle for them. People sense that a seven is always holding something back and find it hard to completely trust them. Sevens recognize that they are not understood for who they are and that they are somehow disconnected from other people. As a consequence, they make a concerted effort to choose their words carefully. In their minds, they will rehearse what they are going to say, so many times, that they become confused and wonder if they have verbalized their thoughts or not. This is clearly a double bind for the very sensitive, shy seven who is struggling not to be misunderstood one more time.

KEY IMAGE: INTROVERT

Their struggle to feel connected to people is complicated by their intrinsic nature to be introverted. By definition, an introvert doesn't express in an outward direction. Communication is like throwing a football with a sender and a receiver. Sevens go through the motion of throwing the ball but instead of letting go at the appropriate moment, they hold on and jam the ball into their stomach.
The other person never gets to receive their message.

Sevens feel claustrophobic around large groups of people. If they work in an office, they spend most of the day waiting to escape to the privacy and quiet of their own home. When they do get home, they are immediately lonely and turn the radio on to fill up the empty spaces. Sevens can be the life of the party one minute and in the next minute a mood will come over them so strongly that they will retreat to their room where they will escape into a book. They are avid readers, to say the least.

Sevens inner search to know why life exists affords them superb analytical skills in science, philosophy, and psychology. They are particularly attracted to the mysteries of electricity and psychic phenomena.

SENSE METAPHOR: SPIRIT

The seventh sense is synonymous with the seventh chakra which is called the crown chakra and denotes our spiritual connection.

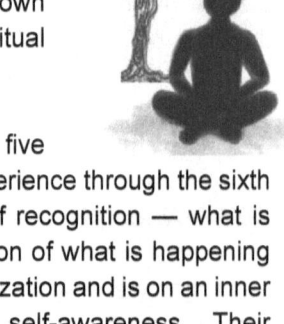

After people experience life through the five physical senses, and interpret their experience through the sixth sense of mind, there comes a point of recognition — what is happening out in the world is a reflection of what is happening within. The seven has come to this realization and is on an inner spiritual journey of self-discovery and self-awareness. Their self-awareness is often interpreted by themselves and others as self-consciousness. This is true if they identify their lives by external rather than internal values.

Sevens, in tune with themselves, realize that all of the spiritual answers lie within, with the Inner Self, the Inner Child who is deeply in touch with the feeling tones of life. Feeling tones are expansive and powerful, indeed. They can override all the logic of words and can dramatically alter our five physical senses. Sevens are deeply aware of feelings which are far more expansive than words. Consequently, they spend a great deal of their time in a quandary about what they feel. In truth, they feel and sense many things that most of us never know. They feel the pulsation of life, they can talk to the trees and to the animals. To sevens, trees are but slow moving people — trees are alive and have a consciousness of their own that must be respected and appreciated.

The deep sensitivities of the seven offer them a rich sensual, sexual nature which they can enjoy immensely. Intimacy and vulnerability live in contradiction to their intrinsic introverted nature. Consequently, delicate intimate times are short-lived before they retreat to the privacy of their own being. The time frames between intimate, personal contact can be long indeed. This poses a difficult challenge to their partners who, in the midst of being totally enthralled with the beauty of the seven's vulnerability, are suddenly left with a sense of total abandonment while the seven claims long periods of private time alone.

Their attunement to the energy of the Inner Child assists them with appearing younger than their physical age by as much as ten or twenty years. Their appearance portrays youth, innocence, and peace. Sevens can have a very stoic, placid appearance, even when they have been deeply hurt by an unkind remark. Their silence can be the only indication of their hurt. Ask them what's wrong when you know they are hurt or angry and they will very flatly say, "Nothing." Their silence can be awesome and disconcerting, to say the least. If they decide to punish with their silence, they can be relentless and maintain a penetrating, hurtful silence for years, if not a lifetime.

Sevens have very distinctive eyes which are large, elongated, and oval shaped. Egyptian statues depict the style of a seven's eyes.

Other symbols of the seven are the Seven Doors, the Seven Candles, and the Seven Veils. Their search for the inner truth leads them into philosophy and religion where they hold deep convictions.

The essence of spirit is directly related to the breath of life. Respiration comes from the root of re-spirit, expiration from the root of exit-the-spirit. Sevens are sensitive in the lung area of the body. They are subject to chest colds and pneumonia.

They are sensitive to all the subtleties of their environment, including people and the elements. They dislike cold weather and adore hot, sunny days. It's easy to identify a seven on a cold day — they will be shaking like a leaf from the cold and their jacket will be wide open. Ask them why they don't button their jacket and they will respond with, "I'm just fine, thank you." They dislike confinement so much that even buttoning up their coat is a restriction to the freedom of their spirit. You can well imagine how much they like elevators and crowds of people! They adore the out-of-doors and nature.

Sevens have a love-hate relationship with sleeping. They adore the freedom that their spirit has when their physical body sleeps. They cherish their rich dream life and, at the same time, their dreams often scare the life out of them. Their dreams are so totally unique and different, that they are absolutely certain that if they shared them with anyone, they would be committed to a mental institution. Even a seven's very best friend does not know their deepest dreams or their deepest feelings. Besides, both their deepest dreams and feelings transcend words. Sevens often wonder if they will come back to their body in the morning or if this is the last night that they will bid a goodnight to the world.

Sevens have an extremely sensitive solar plexus that flutters whenever they get at all nervous. Many sevens live with a constant palpitation in their solar plexus. It feels like butterflies in the stomach and can be very uncomfortable. People very strong in the seven quality have the feeling of butterflies from childhood and are surprised to be told that not everyone has the same experience. Often, the feeling is confused with an ulcerated stomach which no amount of medication seems to resolve. Fives also have a very sensitive solar plexus but they experience a turn-key tension rather than a fluttering.

PLANT METAPHOR: BLOSSOM

After the budding stage of growth comes the blossom time of spring. Imagine an apple orchard in blossom on a crystal clear day under a rich blue sky. Sitting in a branch over your head, you notice a robin with a deep orange-red chest singing to the world.  The beauty and grace of it all touches your heart and soul. Words can't capture what you see and feel. Imagine yourself deeply enjoying such an experience when suddenly your reality is shattered by another voice that is compelled to label the mystery and magic of spring with; "Look at the robin. What a beautiful day. Don't you love the spring? Are you having a good day?" Such statements are irrelevant and dramatically disconcerting to a seven.

Blossoms are very delicate. During this period, if it's too hot, too cold, too wet, too rainy, or the blossom is not fertilized, the apple tree will not bear fruit. The delicate nature of the seven needs to be honoured if the next step of growth is to be experienced.

ASTROLOGY METAPHOR: LIBRA

Libra is native to the seventh house of the Zodiac and represents the beginning of refinement and the process of truly exploring relationships. Libra seeks a higher sense of sociability amongst family and friends.

They are idealistic, sensitive, and not fully conscious of the nature of relationship, yet eager to explore and discover the gentle currents of interrelatedness. Libra seeks the delicate balance between self and others.

Like sevens, Libras seek tranquillity and peace at all costs and often sacrifice themselves in the name of relationship — particularly during the first half of a relationship. The challenge of Libra is not to be so preoccupied with other people that they lose their own centre and their own voice. Their preoccupation can give way to indecisiveness. In this sense, they can have trouble with boundaries and lack a sense of purpose and practical application.

Libra has a gift of being able to see the essence of people. They are very skilled at questioning people. In the business world, Libra is outstanding at interviewing and hiring the right people for the right job.

Libra is an air sign and is not good at being embodied and grounded. Their relationship to love, beauty, and harmony is refined, abstract, and ethereal. They have a well developed ability to internalize, seeking spiritual truths and fairness. They are very aware that relationships must include a spiritual focus, and for relationships to work, a spiritual balance must be maintained.

Sevens adore the sensual experience of close relationships and at the same time fear the vulnerability and intimacy that comes hand-in-hand with such experiences. Their tendency is to give themselves away, to compromise themselves as Libras do. Neither Libra nor a seven will ever forget an emotional slight and will remind their partner of such events many years later — and in exacting detail.

Like sevens, Libras are intellectual and actively seek knowledge, new ideas, and mental stimulation. They are very adept at analyzing life and all matters of psychology and human relationships.

Both Libra and sevens seldom express their anger. Yet, when they do, it leaves them shaken and physically ill.

CHAPTER 8 — QUALITIES OF THE EIGHT

Within the four metaphors, the qualities of the EIGHT are:

PEOPLE	PLANTS	SENSES	ASTROLOGY
ADMINISTRATOR	FRUITION	GROUNDING	SCORPIO

PEOPLE METAPHOR: ADMINISTRATOR

As single people, we primarily live for ourselves. When we marry, life becomes much more of a give-and-take affair. Life changes radically when the firstborn arrives home with feedings and diaper changes at all times of the day and night. The notion of "being of service" to the infant and to life becomes a reality that can be the greatest joy and the greatest heartache, both at the same time.

Eights understand service and are natural administrators. They know how to delegate and base their decisions on the end results. The best excuse in the world will not change the mind of an eight. To an eight, only results speak of what the true intention was. For this reason, they are seen as having very thick skin. When they are accused of being unfeeling and inflexible, they don't understand. In their experience, they are very finely tuned. Eights capitalize on the feelings that the seven experiences to discern the truth of what is happening in their world. Mind you, they seldom admit to being sensitive. Rather, they call it their street sense, their gut instinct, or their business sense. It's all the same — it's being tuned to what is truly going on without any embellishments. What are the facts and what will it take to get the job done? Eights are shrewd, discerning and very thorough.

Eights can become bored with ordinary life because they are particularly competent at creating wealth. When this happens, they sometimes pursue the challenge of criminal activity to keep themselves entertained. An eight who makes such a choice can be particularly unscrupulous and dishonest.

Criminal activity is quite opposite to the natural keynote of the eight, who has a deep instinct for justice. Hence, as it is with all qualities, there are two sides to the coin for eights: justice or exploitation.

Administrators of companies are concerned with both quality and quantity in order to generate the best possible, bottom-line profits. In keeping with this attitude, eights are most comfortable with both quality and quantity in all areas of their lives; food, drink, sex, homes, clothes, and all manner of possessions. They are prone to being overweight because of their love for rich, gourmet foods. They are uncomfortable unless they can travel first class and stay at the best hotels. Quality material objects touch their hearts, especially art and sculpture. Eights sense a communion with the divine when they experience or come in contact with quality.

Their appreciation of quality attracts life to them. Consequently, rather than pursue life, they allow life to come to them. They intrinsically believe that they are deserving of all manner of material abundance.

Highly efficient administrators are usually in the position of approving activities rather than offering lengthy descriptions of what they want done. They listen intently and will often express their approval with a simple nod of their head. Although it is their tendency not to talk very much or very often, their sense of authority demands that when they do talk, you are well advised to listen without the slightest interruption.

If you owe an eight $100, they completely expect the full amount to be repaid. Eights will be extremely indignant if you return $95 and suggest that $5 is neither here nor there between friends. Yet, on the other hand, if the full $100 is repaid graciously, they are prone to immediately give the $100 back as a gift. You must first keep the original agreement before they will be charitable.

A predominant focus of men and women, who are eights, is producing external, material results. An over-emphasis of external results is out of harmony with the internal, female reproductive organs and can cause complications with the menstrual cycle and childbearing. Males overly focused on the material aspects of life are subject to infections and cancer of the prostate, testicles, and bladder.

In general, men tend to be overly absorbed in their careers. It is particularly a struggle for eights to maintain a balance with their home and family. After years of superbly providing for material needs, they can come home one evening to a home with no wife, children or furniture and be completely perplexed as to why. On the other hand, eights can be particularly sensitive to maintaining a balance if they use their innate sense of the truth to discern what is needed to maintain the equanimity of a mature home environment.

Eights have a very dignified, erect walk. It appears that their entire upper body is rigid and only their legs move.

PLANT METAPHOR: FRUITION

The eighth stage of growth is symbolized by the apple attached to the tree – mature, ripe, succulent, and deep red in colour. This is the peak of the fruition cycle and is the end result of all the growth stages from seed, sprouting, first leaf, roots, rapid growth, budding and blossoming. To the farmer, it represents material success and money. As a society, we set aside a day of Thanksgiving to reflect on and express appreciation for the bounties that our earth provides. This is especially meaningful when we are the caretakers of the fields and orchards. So it is with the eight who embraces all of the qualities from one through seven, plus appreciation and caring for our material earth. The fruition only comes to pass with balance, harmony, and a deep communion with Mother Earth. All stages and all ingredients must be justly embraced to cultivate succulent apples that will command the best possible price in the market.

SENSE METAPHOR: GROUNDING

After one experiences life through the five physical senses, and interprets their experience through the sixth sense of mind, there comes a point of recognition that what is happening out there in the world is a reflection of what is happening within. This awareness earmarks the beginning of the spiritual journey within. In the process of waking-up spiritually, it is common for people to become very inspired about transformation, spiritual growth, transcendence, and ascendance. Many say, *"Count me in — I want to be One with God — beam me up Scotty!!"*. In their enthusiasm, they forget that the spiritual secrets lie within, through self-discovery and self-awareness, as opposed to outside of themselves. The journey is "through the earth" versus ascending off the face of the earth. The secret is a willingness to be here, on earth, and to embrace all life in its hues of light and dark. In other words, the last spiritual secret is grounding, being here now, keeping both feet firmly on the ground.

Eights acknowledge that spirituality is about being of the earth, rather than escaping from the earth. They embrace life rather than avoid the polarities, contradictions, and paradoxes of life. Their ability to resolve conflict is excellent because they recognize there are an infinite number of solutions to any given problem.

Options are a hallmark of expanding consciousness and dissolving limiting belief systems. In contrast, when we become stuck and hold onto positions, our vision has become restricted to focusing on a single option and we have lost sight of all other possibilities.

Eights are good administrators, and get paid handsomely, because they don't get stuck on positions. In the face of crises, they stay calm, flexible, and trust their knowing that for every problem there are many solutions. Other qualities prefer the drama of right or wrong, good or bad, my way or the highway. Notice the difference — the eight thinks in terms of this and that versus this or that.

Eights are finely attuned spiritually. They instinctively bring the spiritual energy of life down into their body and anchor it in the earth below the feet. Therefore, the eight experiences the eighth chakra below the feet in the ground, whereas other qualities will experience this chakra above the head or at different levels within the physical body. Because eights sense the eighth chakra under their feet, they are very conscious of what style and quality of shoe they and other people wear. Shoes can become a fetish for eights and they may buy a new pair of very expensive shoes every month, if not more often.

One ancient myth places the eight on a marble throne which sits upon a bed of marble and surrounded by a pool of mercury. It's a place of perfect stillness and reflection with a full view of the entire universe. Having discovered all the spiritual secrets of life and applied them to everyday living, the eight is able to reflect on the perfection of the universe.

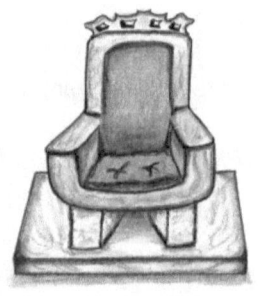

It is apparent to eights that life is a gift and it's their responsibility to willingly accept the fruits of the universe. Consequently, eights are not inclined to pursue life. They center themselves in an inner space of nirvana and allow life to come to them. When eights surrender to this place of nirvana, they blend with the quality of the nine which is the full and complete self on the physical plane.

ASTROLOGY METAPHOR: SCORPIO

Scorpio is ruled by Pluto and is natal to the eighth house of the Zodiac. Both Scorpio and Pluto activate the deepest and most profound transformative changes possible.

Unlike Libra who seeks a blissful union, Scorpio seeks the embrace of opposites and an acceptance of separateness. Scorpio sees the process of death and rebirth as a natural cycle of nature. Each time they descend into the realm of material form, the underworld, the unconscious, and experience death, they emerge with another philosopher's stone, a piece of themselves.

There is an evolution through the signs and the numbers. By the time we get to eight, there is a clear, integral focus of self and others that allows the deepest desires and passions to manifest. They have the ability to move great currents of energy in the name of accomplishing their dreams.

Scorpio represents an in-depth dialogue of opposites — life and death, good and bad, black and white. Even the number eight, which is a symbol of infinity turned upright, is a symbol of a dialogue. As in the symbol of infinity, polar opposites are connected and are equal. Scorpio understands the illusion of the apparent polarization of opposites. The life lesson of Scorpio is surrendering their control and trusting that their dark impulses are not bad, but rather a mistranslation of passion. Scorpio has a tremendous ability to focus their passion, transform energy, heal others, and manifest their desires.
Scorpio rules the genitals which symbolize procreation and

re-creation. Scorpios are extremely sensitive but don't easily express their feelings. Sexual passion and money are equally important to them. They can be very manipulative, seductive, and coy. They are interested in the bottom line and pursue the truth like the surgeon's knife which unemotionally cuts out what no longer works. There is also a ruthlessness to Scorpio. Nothing gets in their way. They are single-eyed and focused.

Their desire for knowing the truth makes them superb psychiatrists, detectives, surgeons, or administrators. They have x-ray vision and are outstanding listeners. Their quiet, secretive manner can hide an extreme temper that carries the sting of the scorpion.

In Libra, energy begins to move as an intellectual longing for harmony. It's more about a thought process. Whereas, in Scorpio, it's a desire to embody the energy as it becomes far more intense.

Scorpios, like surgeons, are looked upon as people who have lots of power and are often perceived as threatening and scary.

CHAPTER 9 — QUALITIES OF THE NINE

Within the four metaphors, the qualities of the NINE are:

PEOPLE	PLANTS	SENSES	ASTROLOGY
TEACHER	FRUIT DROPS	COMPLETE SELF	SAGITTARIUS

PEOPLE METAPHOR: TEACHER

First, let's review the metaphor of people: man, woman, child, student, traveller, family, philosopher, administrator. An ancient adage says that one can only truly teach what one has experienced. This adage stems from the observation that knowledge is accumulated in the mind, whereas wisdom is infused in the body and comes from successfully living life. There is a delicate, fine line between responsible teaching that offers choices and a saviour attitude that meddles in the affairs of others. The nine embraces all the qualities from one through eight and is in the ultimate position to teach about the essence of life.

KEY IMAGE: HUMANITARIAN

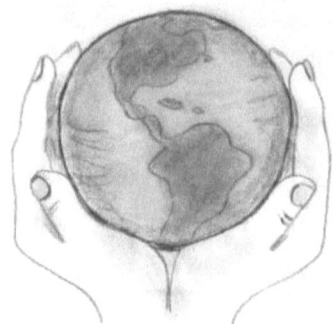

Nines are truly humanitarian. They constantly seek to promote the welfare of humankind and strive to eliminate pain and suffering. They are extremely compassionate and generous. Typically, they give away more than they can afford and experience a deep sadness for not being able to give more. Their finely tuned nervous systems readily respond to the hurts and feelings of others. For example, a man strong in the nines, may have serious bouts of morning sickness when his wife is pregnant. If they don't learn to set boundaries, they can suffer from serious nervous system disorders.

Nines hold the highest of spiritual ideals and can fall into the trap of being perfectionists if they lose their practical sense, their grounding. Spiritual ideals are founded on letting go, forgiveness, and unconditional love. Nines must learn this lesson in its finest shadings. They are much more finely tuned than the other numbers and simply are not allowed the grace of much latitude for margin of error. This "fact" can bother them substantially. If they are the slightest bit possessive, they quickly lose those things that they cherish and love the most. Without a spiritual focus and an outlet for their creativity, nines become laden with self-pity and possessiveness. When caught in such qualities, they give vent to an uncontrolled temper and extreme jealousy.

They are most content when they can give to others. Often, they will fulfil their perfectionist and spiritual ideals by becoming specialists in various professions, particularly in the medical field. Nines are best suited to teaching in inspirational and creative professions rather than in hard-nosed, material business arenas. Their sympathetic and compassionate nature is prone to being too compromising and they will minimize their profits in order to give their clients an exceptional deal.

Nines can be extremely high-strung and inspired. They can be like a butterfly, moved by unseen and unfelt currents of wind. They love everything and everyone. They are highly creative in music and all of the arts. Their verbal skills are excellent and they adore an abundance of gentle, physical contact — they are very loving.

PLANT METAPHOR: FRUIT DROPS

When an apple is left to ripen on the tree, nature will eventually take her course and the apple will drop to the ground, suffering a bruise or two in the process. Unless man interferes, one of two things will happen. Either, an animal eats the apple and assists the tree by carrying the seeds some distance before they are excreted to begin the process of growth anew. Or, the apple deteriorates on the spot, fertilizing the soil and enhancing the seed's chances of taking root. In either case, the apple relinquishes itself in order for the process of growth to begin anew. Similarly, the nine is asked to give back to the process of life, whereas all the other numbers draw from the earth to create the seeds within the apple.

The image of the ripe and fallen apple emphasizes the qualities of the nine: completion, surrender, letting go, and unconditional love. These qualities go hand-in-hand with humanitarian instincts and forgiveness. The challenge for the nine is to resist completely surrendering their lives to the needs of others and live as martyrs. The highest spiritual ideals include doing the first works first, which means attending to one's personal needs before addressing the needs of others. No one can be a philanthropist if they have nothing to give. This is true also for qualities such as compassion and love.

SENSE METAPHOR: COMPLETE SELF

The ninth chakra represents the full potentiality of the human experience on the physical plane. The ninth chakra is superseded by the tenth chakra which is the Future Self, the eleventh which is the Soul, the twelfth which is the Higher Self, and the thirteenth which is Christ/Buddha Consciousness or the equivalent. Just as the eight instinctively brings the spiritual energy down into the body and grounds it, the nine instinctively brings the succeeding levels of spiritual energy into the physical body to experience the richest, possible joy of living. However, this means embracing both sides of the coin — the good and the bad, the light and the dark — without judgement, yet with discernment and a willingness to feel pure love without resistance or defence. These are gracious and desirable ideals that are mastered by few.

ASTROLOGY METAPHOR: SAGITTARIUS

The ninth house of the Zodiac is Sagittarius, ruled by Jupiter which is the largest planet. They represent the expansion of consciousness following the Scorpion's descent into darkness, the unconscious.

They embody higher levels of understanding, intellectual development, the wisdom of the shaman, and the spiritual teacher. Their deepest desire is to understand the abstract and teach a philosophy of life.

As perpetual students, they seek the bigger picture of life and have an opinion on everything. They are in love with the spirit of life and want to be with lots of people all the time. Sagittarians desire everything on a huge scale, they love freedom and the out-of-doors where they can run.

The more refined side of Sagittarius is a sense of real optimism. When their optimistic spirit is at hand, their communication comes with a lovely sense of humour that invites you to gladly listen to the truth like you have never heard it before. Sagittarius has the ability to see the bigger picture, laugh in the face of failure, laugh in the face of success, be unimpressed with any of it, and be impressed with all of it. They are full of laughter and joy.

On the negative side, they can be brutally honest without any tact. When they are in this dogmatic, self-righteous state, they won't listen to others, insisting on learning only from their own experience. Sagittarius can be very righteous and has a tendency to be extremely opinionated, blunt, and forthright without inhibition. Particularly in matters that count.

Sagittarians will often indulge in alcohol, food, and drugs. They can be considered loud, gregarious, and indulgent. Sagittarians can be party animals who love to feel the movement of spirit.

Nine is the completion of the numbers in a physical sense which reflects in the nature of Sagittarians who love to complete, reach the goal, and run in the pursuit of wisdom. Where Scorpio is the collector of philosopher's stones through the process of death and resurrection, Sagittarius is the collector of philosopher's stones through the joy of learning.

Sagittarians can be burdened with a feeling that there is no where for them to rest. Since life is a path of change and nothing stays the same, they are constantly forced to let go. They are always packing their bags and, once more, they are on the move. However, it is the luckiest sign of the Zodiac, because they embrace a spiritual sense of destiny and sincere optimism.

CAPRICORN, AQUARIUS, & PISCES

In drawing this parallel between the houses of astrology and the numbers from one to nine, many ask how the 10th, 11th, and 12th houses of the Zodiac relate. The numbers 10, 11, and 12 reduce to 1, 2, and 3 and represent the beginning of the next octave of nine. They are the future personalities where 10 = Future Self, 11 = Soul, 12 = Higher Self and 13 = Christ Consciousness. In this sense, they are not as colored with personality. In fact, Capricorn is known as the sign that doesn't have a personality.

Capricorn, Aquarius and Pisces are known as the three eccentrics in astrology and truly draw from abstract realms in comparison to the first nine signs which depict the evolution of life from a raw burst of primal energy to the full integration of the

Self in physical form.

Appendix 'A' is a delightful, short story that reviews the evolution of the Zodiac signs. It is presented in the appendix for those who are astrology fans and would enjoy a tantalizing short story that captures the essence of each of the signs.

CHAPTER 10 — POSITIVE VERSUS NEGATIVE TRAITS

Consistent with the basic nature of all life which embraces duality, polarity, and paradox, each of the numbers reflect both sides of a coin — one side being positive and the other side being negative. The choice of which side we express and when, is an individual, moment to moment decision.

Although the first 9 chapters capture the basic qualities of the numbers, the focus was primarily on the positive aspects of each number. The following table is a summary of both positive and negative traits of the numbers.

POSITIVES: **NEGATIVES:**

ONE
individualistic, original, wilful, independent, persevering, candid, bold, pragmatic, initiating, active

domineering, aggressive, unmovable, self-centered, egotistical, blunt, unfeeling, isolated, antisocial

TWO
diplomatic, tactful, charming, intuitive, sensitive, persuasive, cooperative, considerate, adaptable, mediating, nurturing, receptive, affectionate, good-natured

procrastinating, passive, lazy, careless, impractical, gullible, indecisive, indifferent, petty, shy, fearful, dependent, self-delusion

THREE
extroverted, entertaining, artistic, magnetic, generous, musical, cheerful, optimistic, gregarious, cosmopolitan, articulate, passionate, imaginative, creative, flair, style, well-dressed

introverted, argumentative, emotional drama, unfocused, frivolous, superficial, vain, extravagant, gossipy, whining, gaudy

POSITIVES:

FOUR
analytical, practical, productive, organized, precise, focused, intellectual, reliable, disciplined, patient, persevering, honest, punctual, trustworthy, loyal, prudent, traditional, rooted

FIVE
expansive, promotional, versatile, self-reliant, decisive, curious, enthusiastic, enterprising, freedom loving, adventurous, insightful, vitality, aliveness, assertive, non-conformist, progressive, courageous

SIX
responsible, accountable, sensible, paternal, maternal, affectionate, artistic, wise, congenial, stable, balanced, harmonious, home and community minded, counsellor

SEVEN
introspective, inquisitive, reflective, calm, refined, poised, dignified, poetic, philosophical, insightful, spiritually attuned, mystical, sensual

NEGATIVES:

disorganized, unproductive, lack ambition, discontent, sceptical, narrow-minded, fussy, rigid, dogmatic, stubborn, dull, slow, plodding, penny-pincher, limited, restricted

contracted, critical, moody, chaotic, cruel, temperamental, contemptuous, callous, bitter, aggressive, compulsive, indulgent, impatient, intolerant, drifter, suicidal, naive,

interfering, bossy, irresponsible, obstinate, opinionated, confused, unfocused, worrywart, faultfinding

secretive, repressed, jealous, ungrounded, disconnected, pessimistic, aloof, nervous, fearful, moody, tactless, crude, antisocial, complete introversion

POSITIVES:	NEGATIVES:
EIGHT administrative, just, confident, discriminating, shrewd, balanced, stable, ambitious, authoritative, leadership oriented, thorough, efficient, results-oriented, material appreciation, material success, prosperity, abundance, benevolent, charitable	unscrupulous, miserly, calculating, fatalistic, materialistic, domineering, power-hungry, oppressive, manipulative, exploitive, revengeful, impatient
NINE humanitarian, altruistic, unconditional love, forgiving, intuitive, musical, artistic, visionary, inspirational, generous, compassionate, empathic, tolerant	self-pitying, jealous, possessive, unforgiving, uncontrolled temper, quitters, smothering, sacrificing, selfish, aimless dreaming, idealistic, emotional extremes

THE ODD NUMBERS — 1-3-5-7-9

Generally speaking, they are active in nature and relate to thoughts and ideas. They are intuitive, inspirational and artistic. Although the one is not artistic in a musical sense, they are very creative in a pioneering and survival sense.

THE EVEN NUMBERS — 2-4-6-8

Generally speaking, they are more passive in nature and relate to practical realities. They are analytical, materialistic, and reserved.

CHAPTER 11 — METAPHORS & KEYWORDS

This chapter is a summary of the metaphors and keywords used to create word pictures to define the qualities of the numbers. See the following page for a table.

The astrological metaphor was presented in the previous chapters to complement the qualities of the numbers and to highlight the common thread between all the oracles which identify the human journey. For those who are fans of astrology, a delightful, short story is presented in Appendix "A" that reflects the evolution of consciousness through the houses of the Zodiac. Appendix "B" repeats the following table and includes an astrological reference and health considerations discussed in Chapter 24.

PLANT	HUMAN	SENSES	KEYWORDS
1. Seed	Male	Touch	Pioneer, Initiating, Independent
2. Sprouting	Female	Taste	Diplomat, Bonding, Relationships
3. First Leaf	Child	Smell	Entertainer, Extrovert, Expressive
4. Roots	Student	Hearing	Analyzer, Technician, Details
5. Rapid Growth	Traveller	Sight	Promoter, Transformation, Change
6. Budding	Family	Mind	Counsellor, Sensible, Accountable
7. Blossom	Philosopher	Spirit	Poet, Stoic, Introvert
8. Ripe Apple	Administrator	Grounding	Results, Justice, Service
9. Apple Drops	Teacher	Complete/ Full-Self	Humanitarian, Completion, Surrender, Letting Go

The above qualities can be subdivided into three groups as follows:

1-2-3	Physical	or	Seeding
4-5-6	Mental	or	Cultivation
7-8-9	Spiritual	or	Fruition

Within each group, the qualities follow a secondary pattern of physical, mental, and spiritual focus as follows:

PHYSICAL	1 = physical	focus in the physical group
	2 = mental	focus in the physical group
	3 = spiritual	focus in the physical group
MENTAL	4 = **mental**	focus in the mental group **
	5 = **physical**	focus in the mental group **
	6 = spiritual	focus in the mental group
SPIRITUAL	7 = physical	focus in the spiritual group
	8 = mental	focus in the spiritual group
	9 = spiritual	focus in the spiritual group

**

Note: The sequence of physical, mental, and spiritual does not follow the same order in this group.

COMPATIBILITY GROUPS

This secondary pattern of physical, mental, and spiritual qualities forms the compatibility groups. The numbers in each group share the same basic nature:

1-5-7 PHYSICAL These numbers are independent, self-sufficient, and detached from people. They have a strong physical connection with the earth and like to work at making ideas concrete and physically real. People strong in these numbers don't take advice well ... they insist on working it out themselves. It takes time for them to embody (integrate or absorb) new ideas.

2-4-8 MENTAL These numbers are organized, practical, analytical, and technical in nature. They are mediators, coordinators, and administrators — they are the liaison between the spiritual and the physical group. They think and conceptualize best when they are talking.

3-6-9 SPIRITUAL These numbers are inspirational, playful, and idealistic. Their focus is purely conceptual — they are idea people who need help to implement their insights. Their ideas come to them spontaneously, in flashes. They do not need time to sit and reflect like the physical group, nor do they have to talk it out like the mental group. Ideas come in reveries and it frustrates them that others take so long to grasp what is intuitively apparent to them.

The three groups serve life well. The inspirational nature of the spiritual group is attuned to new ideas. The mental group talks the ideas over and fills in the blanks that the spiritual group doesn't have the patience to identify. When the mental group have the ideas clarified and organized, they are able to communicate the concept to the physical group who are adept at making new ideas physical, tangible realities.

The compatibility group to which you belong is determined by your day of birth. If it exceeds 9, do one of the following procedures to reduce the numeric value to a single digit:

A. Repeatedly subtract 9 from the sum until the numeric value becomes 9 or less. Using 22nd of the month as an example;
22 - 9 = 13, 13 - 9 = 4. The desired number is a 4.

or

B. Simply add the individual digits of the number together. Using the example of 22nd of the month, the digits are 2 + 2 = 4.

The compatibility groups form a spectrum from introverted to extroverted with the middle group being a blended/balance point and go-between for the two polarities:

       1-5-7   Introverted

       2-4-8   Blended/Balance

       3-6-9   Extroverted

Although the 7 is the most introspective of all the numbers, the word introvert also applies to the 1 & 5 in the sense that they draw their energy and ideas from within themselves. In comparison, the 3-6-9 have an air of inspiration and draw their ideas and motivation from outside of themselves.

These groups are most useful when determining the level of compatibility between people. People of opposite basic natures (i.e. introverted versus extroverted) do not get along well over an extended period of time. People get along best with those from their same group. The following compatibility considerations apply to each group:

1-5-7 PHYSICAL The Physical group gets along best with others in its own group, not well with those in the mental group, and very poorly with those in the spiritual group.

2-4-8 MENTAL The Mental group gets along best with others in its own group, quite well with those in the spiritual group, and reasonably well with those in the physical group. The mental group acts as the mediator between the physical and the spiritual groups.

3-6-9 SPIRITUAL The Spiritual group gets along best with others in its own group, quite well with those in the mental group, and very poorly with those in the physical group.

It's unwise for people from the physical and spiritual groups to marry. They may uphold the same beliefs and values, yet they arrive at the same destination from two completely different directions. They may share the same goals but not the same journey.

Although the compatibility group is only one of many factors involved in determining overall compatibility, you can discover a great deal about the people you know simply by determining their compatibility group.

A more comprehensive discussion of compatibility factors is presented in Chapter 23. But first, let's take the next easiest step and learn about the 9 Year Cycle which offers some amazing insights into life's process.

PART III

THE 9 YEAR CYCLE OF LIFE

CHAPTER 12 — THE 9 YEAR CYCLE IN SUMMARY

The qualities of the numbers apply to three specific areas: the 9 Year Cycle, names, and birthdates. The easiest of the three to compute and understand is the 9 year cycle. Before we compute your personal cycle and interpret what that means, let's reflect on the nature of cycles.

There are many different cycles in the human experience. Familiar ones are night and day, the four seasons, women's menstrual cycle, the ocean tides. Less familiar cycles are the 21, 28, and 33 day biorhythm cycle, the 29 year Saturn cycle with its 7 year segments, and the 84 year Uranus cycle, to name but a few.

The advantage of knowing the year of your personal cycle within the 9 year span is similar to knowing what season of the year it is. For example, in Vancouver, Canada, it is not a good idea to plan a downhill ski trip to the local mountains in July. It simply will not be a gratifying experience. Planting grass in Alaska in the winter months is ludicrous. Similarly, knowing one's cycle can greatly enhance the odds of success in any given season.

The 9 year cycle is dictated by the calendar year of January 1st through December 31st. This cycle exists because we have a collective consciousness of a calendar year made up of 365 days and beginning on January 1st. If our consensual reality was different than a 365 day year, our experience of this 9 year cycle would vary accordingly. In comparison, all the astrology cycles influence one's life from the day of birth plus 365 days.

COMPUTING YOUR CYCLE YEAR

Your current cycle year is computed by adding the following factors together:

>   month of birth + day of birth + the current year + one

For example, if you were born on April 22 and the current year is 1990, compute your cycle year for the calendar year 1990 as follows:

month of birth	+	day of birth	+	current year	+	one
April	+	22	+	1990	+	1
4	+	4	+	1	+	1
= 10 = 1 year						

When a number or the sum of a series of numbers exceeds 9, do one of the following procedures to reduce the numeric value to a single digit:

A. Repeatedly subtract 9 from the sum until the numeric value becomes 9 or less. Let's use 22 as an example; 22 - 9 = 13, 13 - 9 = 4. The desired number is a 4.

or

B. Simply add the individual digits of the number together. Using the example of 22, the digits are
2 + 2 = 4.

Consider the example of someone born on September 4 and the current year is 1991. Their cycle year in 1991 would be:

month of birth	+	day of birth	+	current year	+	one
September	+	4	+	1991	+	1
9	+	4	+	2	+	1
= 16 = 7 year						

Remember to use the current year in the computation and **not** the year of birth.

Why does the computation include a **plus one**? When a child is born, they live for 365 days before their first birthday. On their first birthday they become 1 year old and begin living their 2nd year of life. The computation of **plus one** compensates for the difference between how many years have passed and in what year we are living.

The notion of **plus one** is not common to numerology. Possibly the differences in approach are a function of the descriptions applied to the cycle years. I find the **plus one** system particularly poignant when the key months outlined in the next chapter are considered. I suggest that you give full consideration to Chapter 13 before you decide for yourself if the computation should be **plus one** or not **plus one**.

THE 9 YEAR CYCLE OF GROWTH

The 9 year cycle can best be defined by the metaphor of the growth of a plant as defined in the first 9 chapters of this book.

THE 9 YEAR CYCLE OF GROWTH

1. Seed   )
2. Sprouting   ) SEEDING
3. First Leaf   )

4. Roots   )
5. Rapid Growth   ) CULTIVATION
6. Budding   )

7. Blossom   )
8. Ripe Apple   ) FRUITION
9. Apple Drops   )

Notice that the 9 year cycle is broken into 3 segments of seeding, cultivation and fruition. Each fruition contains the seeds for the next cycle of growth which unfolds in an ascending spiral of expanding experiences.

Each cycle year forms a bell shaped curve beginning with gentle definition, growing to full intensity in the month of July, and waning to a minimal influence in December. In some cycles, the energy of the cycle peaks in July, and in other cycles, the energy of the cycle is at a minimum in July.

The qualities of each cycle year are identical to the qualities of the numbers as they were defined in chapters 1 through 9.

The following two pages offer a brief summary of each cycle year within the 9 year cycle.

THE 9 YEAR CYCLE IN SUMMARY

The **1 cycle year** is male energy, the pioneer, the seed. During a 1 cycle year, people are independent, candid, bold, practical, initiating, persevering and original. The first 5 months of a 1 cycle year can be agitating, undefined and up-in-the-air.  June, July and August are exceptional times for beginning new ventures and making major life decisions.

The **2 cycle year** is female energy, relationships and sprouting of the seed. During a 2 cycle year, people are concerned with diplomacy, tactfulness, mediating, nurturing and bonding. During this period, they are sensitive,  responsive, cooperative, considerate, adaptable and persuasive. The 2 cycle year is about building relationships and gently resolving differences.

The **3 cycle year** is the child, the extrovert, the first leaf. During the first 7 months of a 3 cycle year, people are cheerful, optimistic, gregarious, cosmopolitan, articulate, imaginative, artistic, musical, entertaining and magnetic. The last 5 months of a 3 year fall flat and feel like a rude letdown as the external growth stops while the plant turns its attention towards the root system.

The 4 cycle year is about education, the analyzer, the root system. During this period, people are plagued with endless picky detail and tested from all corners. They feel weighted down and are slow to make decisions.  This is a time to attend to all of the details, to be totally practical, to get organized and to stick with the status quo. This is clearly not a time to make major decisions or commitments.

The 5 cycle year is about change, travel and rapid growth. Making major changes before July of a 5 cycle year is premature and highly not recommended. During a 5 year, people are self-reliant, independent, adventurous,  versatile, promotional, enterprising, curious and impatient. July and August are exceptional months for making major life changes.

The 6 cycle year is about home, family, and procreation. It's a time of budding. During a 6 cycle year, people are paternal, maternal, sensible, accountable, responsibable,  congenial, and strive to put their house in order. It's a time of taking responsibility for one's life, home, family, relationships and career. Financially, this is an expensive year.

The 7 cycle year is about introspection, spiritual awareness, new energies, blossoming. The first 6 months of a 7 cycle year are disorienting, confusing,  ungrounded, sensitive, vulnerable and highly self-conscious as a whole new level of energy enters the body. This is a time for introspection, self-analysis, meditation and retreat. June can be a most difficult month. During July, the new energies will become stable and open the door to 18 months of fruition and insight.

The 8 cycle year is about fruition, the ripe apple, a time of material rewards. During an 8 cycle year, people are confident, discriminating, shrewd, materially focused, ambitious, authoritative,  results-oriented and feel empowered. Everyone reaps both the good and the bad of what they have sown during the seeding cycle. The negative seeds will particularly manifest in March and April of the 8 year.

The 9 cycle year is about completion, letting go, forgiveness, unconditional love. During a 9 cycle year, people are sensitive, compassionate, empathic, vulnerable, inspirational,  visionary, ungrounded and physically exhausted. The first 7 months of a 9 year are a **review** of the prior 8 years. It's a time of reflection and completion of life to date. The last 5 months are a **preview** of the future.

Do not begin major, new ventures during the last 5 months of a 9 cycle year.

UNSETTLED VS PROGRESSIVE PERIODS

U = UNSETTLED   VU = VERY UNSETTLED
P = PROGRESSIVE   VP = VERY PROGRESSIVE

YEAR	JANUARY – JUNE	JULY - DECEMBER
1	U	VP* *Include June 19 - 30
2	P	P
3	P* *Include July 1 - 18	U
4	VU	VU
5	U	VP
6	P	P
7	U* *Include July 1 - 18	P
8	VP	VP
9	U	P

The 3 cycle year is optimistic for the first half and a let-down in the second half.

The 1, 5, 7, & 9 years are unsettled and disorienting during the first half and progressive during the second half. Although the 9 cycle year is rich with future possibilities during the last 5 months, this is **not a time to begin major, new ventures.**

The 2, 4, 6, & 8 years are relatively steady for the entire year.

Notice that all the even numbers are consistent throughout their perspective year. Whereas, all the odd numbers swing from down to up, except the 3 year which swings from up to down.

A SPECIAL NOTE:

In a nutshell, this chapter has outlined the qualities of each cycle year, whereas the following chapter discusses each year in detail. You may find it interesting to review in detail your current cycle year and then skip to Chapter 14 which explains how to compute and analyze name combinations. Experience is the best teacher, and I believe that the more you get involved with computations and practicing new skills, the more enthused you will become. On the other hand, I'm not suggesting that the next chapter is unimportant. In fact, people often recognize their personal cycle more readily than the influence of their names and birthdate. For this reason, I find that the 9 year cycle is the best starting point for doing a personal analysis.

It's your choice — read the next chapter now or savour it later.

CHAPTER 13 — THE 9 YEAR CYCLE IN DETAIL

This chapter reviews each year of the 9 year cycle in greater detail than in the previous chapter and makes reference to key months within each year.

1 CYCLE YEAR

All the qualities of the seed, the pioneer, and male energy, outlined in Chapter 1, are applicable to the 1 cycle year. The nature of this year is independent, self-sufficient, candid, bold, practical, and initiating. The experiences of this year will be pioneering and related to planting seeds for future harvest in the fruition cycle. Those who are generally shy and retiring can come out of their shells and open themselves to new possibilities. Businesses that have prospered may begin a new division or incorporate a new product line. Relationships that have been on shaky ground will terminate or resolve with a new depth of commitment. A woman who never wears blue jeans, may take everyone by surprise and live in them for some months. Those who like luxury may venture off into the wilderness for a camping holiday for the first time in their lives.

Although the 1, 2, & 3 cycle years are about seeding, the 1 cycle year is the **key time** for beginning major new projects or making major long-term commitments. Long-term commitments would span periods of 5, 10, 20 years and would include lifetime goals and objectives.

The most specific time for such new beginnings is from June 19th through August 17th. This 2 month period is the most fertile time for planting new seeds in the entire 108 months that constitute the nine year cycle of growth. Within this 2 month period, the 9 days from June 19th through June 27th are particularly significant. The most powerful time of all is the day of June 19th. On this specific day, I strongly encourage you to spend at least 3 hours in the morning writing or rewriting your personal life goals and objectives. Secondly, I encourage you to pay particular attention to what offers may be made to you on this day. If, for example, you are in the computer business and someone proposes a partnership to you on June 19th, and the proposal is in alignment with your goals and objectives, then go for it. Similarly, any offers that come your way between June 19th and August 17th hold the potential to be outstanding for you.

Beginning major new ventures between January 1st and June 19th will be premature. A new venture begun during this time will feel like a dance that started on the wrong foot. Time and time again you will pause and start again. Yet, even when you get on the right foot, the rest of the dance has an unpleasant taste and the true flow remains illusive. Often it's more productive to sit the dance out and wait for a more favourable opportunity. Beginning before June 19th, will result in a major reorganization between January 1st and April 30th of the following year, resulting in a weaker foundation than can be achieved by waiting for the ultimate time frame of June 19th through August 17th.

Waiting for the ultimate starting point is a process of allowing the creative tension to build to a peak. This can be a most trying and difficult process as there is a growing inner and outer demand for action. This tension can create frayed nerves and the climate can be testing from every direction. Once June 19th arrives, and the seed is planted (the new business doors are opened), the challenges of the day are relative to the new business venture. One's focus becomes narrowed to the task at hand and the peripheral detail and related concerns become secondary.

If you do not make major changes in a 1 cycle year, or at least very consciously restate your goals, then mother nature will disrupt your world and force growth in the 2 cycle year, particularly between January 1st and April 30th.

It is important to remember that the 1 cycle year is about preparing the soil and planting the seed. Physical growth begins in the 2 cycle year when the seed sprouts. Consequently, at the end of the 1 cycle year, there may be very little, if any, apparent, tangible results to show for the efforts of planting seeds of long-term goals.

2 CYCLE YEAR

The qualities of the 2 are related to the nature of the female energy. This is the time when the seed sprouts because of its relationship with the earth, water, and the heat of the sun. The 2 cycle year is about building relationships. It's about diplomacy, tact, persuasiveness, cooperation, adaptability, mediation, and nurturing.

After the dynamic and vibrant 1 cycle year, it can feel very much like a tea party where little or nothing is happening but idle chitchat. Often it feels like life is on hold while one waits for everyone else to finish their tea before getting on with the job at hand. Even so, the value of the 2 cycle year should never be underestimated. After all, life is about people and it can be easy to forget that all industry and trade is related to servicing people and their needs.

One's physical energy can be very low in a 2 cycle year and the physical body may require extra sleep. It's typical to gain weight during this year because the body's metabolism is slow and people often indulge in sugars to gain a sense of aliveness.

During this period, people can be continuously cold even during hot summer days. At night, they may cover their bed with as many blankets as they do in the winter. Whatever your goals are, take care not to get "cold feet" in a 2 cycle year when it can be a distinct challenge to be assertive. The easygoing posture of the 2 year can result in memory lapses and poor recall.

All in all, the 2 cycle year is pleasant but relatively uneventful. It is part of the seeding cycle and is an excellent time for building relationships, both personal and business. January 1st through April 30th is a particularly strong period for new beginnings. April often presents more than one outstanding opportunity. Changes which should have been made during the summer of the 1 cycle year, are often forced upon one during the first four months of the 2 year.

3 CYCLE YEAR

The first 6 months of the 3 cycle year are full of optimism, excitement, enthusiasm, and great promise. The second half of the 3 cycle year dies on the vine and invariably ends in great disappointment or, at least, on a definitive downbeat. Why?

The 1 year is about planting the seed. The 2 year is when the seed sprouts and grows towards the surface of the soil. The 3 year is when the plant pokes its nose out of the ground and grows its first leaf. This is a very exciting time when there are some tangible, visible results for all the hard work of the two prior years.

After the first few leaves have grown and the seed's nutrients have been expended, the plant must develop its root system to sustain itself. The creative energy goes from external, visible growth and great optimism to an apparent decline as the focus shifts to the invisible growth under the surface. This shift in focus, from excitement and external to detailed and internal, feels like a letdown and is interpreted as a disappointment.

An exciting period of external growth occurs from January 1st through July 18th. On July 19th, the process of growth begins to shift towards the root system. By December 31st, the focus is entirely underground and out of physical sight. The year ends with a feeling that it has died on the vine.

Although the 1, 2, & 3 cycle years are the seeding years, the most effective and productive period is from:

June 19th of a 1 cycle year until July 19th of a 3 cycle year.

It is most unwise to begin a new business, start a new job, or marry after July 18th of a 3 cycle year. In the novel, *MURDER IN THE CATHEDRAL* by T.S. Eliott, Thomas Becket retorts that *"The greatest treason is to do the right thing for the wrong reason."* It is an equally great treason to do the right thing in the wrong **season**. No one can plant a field of wheat out-of-doors in Alaska in January and experience a harvest. Such efforts are going against common sense and all of nature's laws. Similarly, beginning major new ventures after July 18th of the 3 year is going against nature's laws. After July 18th of the 3 year, it is important to stay with the status quo until July 1st of the 5 cycle year.

4 CYCLE YEAR

By the end of the 3 cycle year, the plant has its first leaf or two, has expended all the energy and food supply of the seed, and has only one or two small roots to support itself. This is a very vulnerable condition to be in. If it is too hot, too cold, too wet, too dry, if the cow steps on it, or eats the new leaves, life is over. You name it, if it can go wrong in a 4 cycle year, it will appear to go wrong. Life will point out your weakness in all areas including home, family, relationships, health, finances, automobiles, work, sports, education, etc, etc. It's a very precise, if not outright picky, time when it is imperative to cross all the "t's" and dot all the "i's". This is a time for growing a root system and learning to stand on one's own two feet. It's a year of hard work, establishing system and order, and attending to endless details. Imagine a root system with several primary roots and many branches, splitting down to infinite numbers of fine, hair-like roots — each little fibre represents another detail that must be attended to for the plant to sustain itself. As much as most of us don't want to acknowledge it, life is built on meticulous detail. The 4 cycle year brings our attention to this fact with inescapable clarity.

The root system develops under the ground and represents the subconscious mind. Any incompatible, loose ends in one's subconscious mind will surface in a 4 cycle year and will have to be resolved. In this sense, the 4 year is a gift — a necessary preamble to the 5 cycle year, which is a year of rapid growth and expansion. The degree to which the root system can spread out and grow strong will dictate how tall and expansive the plant can become in the 5 cycle year.

Another metaphor for the 4 cycle year is to consider the image of the space shuttle on the launching pad and the endless, endless detail that must be checked and rechecked before the shuttle can blast off. Blast off time is July of the 5 cycle year. Overlook one small valve during the checkout phase and the entire shuttle can explode during lift-off.

In truth, the 4 year is a gift that points out the weaknesses that must be resolved so you can capitalize on the rapid growth of the 5 cycle year.

March and December of a 4 year are the most difficult. If March is a disaster, December will be comparatively easy. If March is relatively calm, December can be the most difficult month of the year. It is not typical that both March and December are devastating.

By July, most people will be saying, "Enough is enough, is enough, is enough, already." In reality, if you say 5 or 6 more "is enough" before you add in the "already", the person in the 4 cycle year will know exactly what you mean. By September, people in a 4 year wonder if they are ever gong to feel better and survive the onslaught of challenges. They have now had 13 unhappy months since July 18th of the 3 cycle year and have essentially lost hope of seeing another happy day. On the other hand, they sometimes will start to laugh through their tears by this point because life has become so ridiculous that it appears to be more of a joke than a threat.

The 4 year can feel like walking through mud with oversized rubber boots. With each step the mud cakes to the boots and they get heavier and heavier. Each step becomes drudgery and painful. By the end of a 4 cycle year, people will say, "I've got absolutely nothing to show for it, but if I can survive this last year, I can survive anything." Congratulations are due, for now they are standing on their own two feet with a well developed root system and ready for the rapid growth of the 5 cycle year.

A person with many 4's in their names and date of birth, will be in their element in a 4 cycle year because their nature is comfortable with detail, system, order, and hard work. Other qualities, like 3's and 5's, can have a particularly hard time with a 4 cycle year because their character is so radically different from the qualities of the 4.

5 CYCLE YEAR

Although the 5 cycle year is about rapid growth, branching out, change, travel, and transformation, the first 6 months are a time for caution. Any major changes initiated before July 1st are premature and will not work in your favour. In fact, changes made before July 1st invariably conclude with bitter and sometimes caustic repercussions. The first 6 months are a time to allow the creative tension to build as it was appropriate to do in the 1 cycle year.

Typically, people enter the 5 cycle year greatly relieved to be complete with the 4 year. Unfortunately, January of the 5 year is a testing and difficult month. To their chagrin, the 4 year appears to hang on for one more month. February of the 5 year is a delight. It feels like the sun has come out for the first time in 18 months — since the letdown of the second half of the 3 cycle year. In fact, most people will remark that they had forgotten what a sunny day looked like or felt like, given how dull the prior 18 months had been. At this point, many people are so relieved that the drudgery of the 4 year is over, that they jump the gun and begin new projects.

A vivid but disconcerting metaphor for the 4 cycle year is being locked in a basement full of horse manure and mushrooms. The lights are off and several sadistic people are hidden in and about the mushroom bins. Every time you take a step, someone punches you or you bang into something. In the 5 cycle year, someone turns on the lights and you can see that you are in a basement full of horse manure, mushrooms, and several sadistic people. They're still hitting you, but you are so happy to see what's going on that you don't care as you run for the stairs to get out. The blows still hurt and, in fact, they have taken on a sting like someone is adding salt to the wounds. However, you don't really care because you know, you truly know, that you are going to make it to the stairs and escape the insanity. *In this sense, the 4 cycle year is about survival pains and the 5 cycle year is about growth pains.*

July and August of the 5 cycle year are like reaching the top of the stairs from the basement and bursting out into the sunshine. These 2 months are equal in power and opportunity to the period of June 19th through August 17th in the 1 cycle year. This period can be likened to gaining a second wind and a willingness to continue the race. It is a time when one can plant a second crop and enjoy a harvest as bountiful as the harvest resulting from seeds planted in the 1 cycle year. It's a window offered by nature for reaffirming or reconsidering and redirecting one's efforts.

These two months are 2 of the 4 most opportune months for planting new seeds in the entire 9 year cycle of 108 months. Use them wisely.

Before completing with the 5 cycle year, let's review the first 6 months. January is disappointing because it continues the testing nature of the 4 cycle year. February is a great relief when the sunshine reappears for the first time in 18 months. March, April, and May become progressively better even though they have a mean sting to them. Then, just as you are gaining some confidence that the worst is over, June arrives and nearly destroys you. June is an intense month when Mother Nature makes absolutely certain that we have checked out every single detail on the space shuttle before she allows us to blast off. In this sense, June of a 5 year can be most trying. It feels like being back down in the basement full of mushrooms with the lights out. It's absolutely deflating and terribly disconcerting. How does anyone know that they are not entering another 2 years just like they have completed? Emotionally, June can be a devastating experience. Fortunately, July brings confirmation of blast off and life begins anew. The balance of the year is about expansion, promotion, decisions, freedom, adventure and insights.

Once again, July and August of the 5 year are equal in power and opportunity to June 19th through August 17th in a 1 cycle year. If any good offers come your way during these two months and are in line with your goals, take them seriously.

6 CYCLE YEAR

The 6 cycle year is about budding and the beginning of the procreation cycle. It's a very fertile time.

Couples who have been trying to have children for some years, can unexpectedly conceive when one of them is in a 6 cycle year. Similarly, a couple may have a family of teenagers when, to their surprise, they find themselves pregnant after a recess of 10 or 15 years. The 6 cycle year is not a time to take chances around sexuality.

Many people find themselves getting married in a 6 cycle year. The 18 months, from July 18th of the 3 cycle year until February of the 5 cycle year, are typically difficult enough to put most everyone off relationships for life. Then a year of expansion, rapid growth, self-reliance, and love of freedom fosters an attitude of being a committed single. Out of the blue the 6 cycle year arrives, someone just right appears, wedding bells are ringing, and family is on the way. The most surprising element is the committed single who is now deeply contented and has no lingering doubts at all about their choice to marry.

Because the 6 cycle year focuses around marriage, home, and family, it is financially an expensive year. Every day there seems to be an unexpected expense of another 10, 20, or 50 dollars. By the end of the year, one can be very broke, but strangely enough, quite contented.

The 4, 5, & 6 cycle years are a time for cultivation. In other words, the 6 cycle year is still part of the testing period, although, it has little of the sting of the 5 year or the dull drone of the 4 year. It is much the same from beginning to end, although the last half of July can be disappointing and August is definitely a time to attend to details and exercise considerable caution.

One's willingness to be accountable and responsible fosters many insights in a 6 year. It's very much a time for putting one's house in order.

7 CYCLE YEAR

The 7 cycle year begins the 3 year fruition period. Unfortunately, the first 6 months of the fruition cycle are disorienting, confusing, sensitive, vulnerable, and highly self-conscious. Why does the fruition cycle begin with such a strange set of qualities?

The 6 cycle year is the budding cycle, the beginning of the procreation cycle, a time for the conception of new ideas and children. It's a time for putting one's house in order and becoming accountable and responsible for one's environment in anticipation of the arrival of the newborn.

The genuine conception of a new idea will foster a whole flood of ideas and a great inrush of new energy. This is the exact nature of the first half of a 7 cycle year. The crown chakra, the 7th chakra, opens up and in floods an abundance of new energy. The influx of new energy into the crown chakra is initially ungrounded as it permeates the body from the top down. It takes 6 to 7 months for the energy to become reasonably grounded. Ungrounded energy feels disorienting and confusing. For some, the energy can be so intense that it is nauseating and creates dizziness. Physically, this period can be exhausting and extra sleep may be required.

The new energy brings a tremendous amount of attention to one's physical body. From January to July, it feels like you have begun your adolescence all over again. A great deal of time can be spent combing hair, fixing nails, and dressing "just right". It's hard to know which way to turn, what to say, how to stand, or where to sit. People feel terribly conspicuous and cumbersome. The sense of vulnerability can be awesome and frightening. Often people become concerned that they are "losing it" and fear they are going insane. Spending time out-of-doors and in nature will help to alleviate the vulnerability. Your attunement to nature will be very high and rewarding throughout the entire 7 cycle year.

The sense of self-consciousness is interpreted as negative. The desired reaction to the self-consciousness is to foster insights, a healthy sense of self-awareness and introspection. The sense of self-consciousness usually gives way to reclusive behaviour until July when the energy becomes reasonably grounded. The second half of the year continues to be sensitive and vulnerable, although it is much easier to cope with than it is during the first half.

Sometimes the confusion and disorientation only becomes apparent in retrospect. During the fall, one can look back at the spring and be flabbergasted at how unclear and unfocused they were prior to July and are abhorred to reflect on decisions made during this disorienting period.

The new energy builds in intensity as each month passes and is most difficult to cope with in June. For some reason, just before all the pressure is released, rather than hold on for another 10 or 20 days, people will lose their cool, blow up, and quit major jobs or major relationships. June is a most trying and testing time in a 7 cycle year. In this sense, June of a 7 cycle year is like June of a 5 cycle year.

Although the cycle technically turns the corner on July 1st, life doesn't really settle down until after the 18th of July. It is particularly wise to heed the following advice:

DO NOT BEGIN MAJOR NEW PROJECTS DURING THE FIRST HALF OF A 7 CYCLE YEAR.

Once again, let's reflect on why the first half of a 7 cycle year is so unsettled. For something new to materially manifest, the energy of the new idea, concept or event will surface first in the individual's consciousness (6 cycle year) and then in the physical body (7 cycle year). Therefore, the 7 cycle year is the most physical of the 3 cycle years of fruition (7, 8, & 9). The disorientation is a necessary component of the process of manifestation because the energy first permeates the crown chakra and slowly seeps down through the entire physical body. Once the energy becomes fully grounded, the sense of dizziness and disorientation passes. The nauseous, dizzy, and "spacey" feelings are similar to the early stages of pregnancy and the tumescence cycle, or heat cycle for a woman. After the new spiritual energy fully permeates the physical body, the disorientation passes.

By mid-July, the new energy becomes grounded and the second half of the 7 cycle year simply gets better and better. From July of the 7 cycle year until January of the 9 cycle year, i.e. for 18 months, life pays the dividends for the seeding and cultivation years — particularly in a physical and a material sense, whereas the 9 cycle year brings more of a spiritual fruition.

8 CYCLE YEAR

The 8 cycle year is a time of material fruition. It's the time of the ripe, mature apple ready to be picked and enjoyed. Although this period can bring a flood of abundance in many forms, you will reap what you have sown. This law of nature very definitely applies to the 8 cycle year. Although we reap the bad with the good, the unpleasant events will particularly manifest in the last 2 weeks of March and during the month of April of the 8 year. If sufficient negative seeds have been sown, they will continue to mature throughout the entire 8 year.

The peak of the fruition cycle is mid-July through the end of August. The entire year is excellent with the exception of March and April. During the 8 year, people feel like they are "on a roll", that life is finally coming their way. They feel empowered, self-confident, and enjoy an aura of physical well-being. During this period, business deals close easily and to one's advantage.

During an 8 year, the energy focuses in the 8th chakra, which is located below the feet, hence bringing a "grounding" and sense of solidity to one's experience. Even so, the 8 year is not a good time for beginning major new projects that are going to require considerable effort for more than a year. This is because the 9 year is exceptionally low on the scale of physical vitality. Hence, the length of the startup period should be considered carefully when beginning new ventures in the 8 year.

By the end of the 8 year, people can become cocky and start to believe they are invincible. Enjoy the feeling while it lasts because the 9 cycle year will deflate any false sense of empowerment.

9 CYCLE YEAR

The 9 cycle year is the spiritual fruition period. It is the last year of the fruition cycle and is a time of completion, letting go, surrender, forgiveness, and unconditional love. This period is symbolized by the apple falling to the ground and being bruised by the fall. Hopefully, the cow will come by and eat it thereby carrying the seeds a sufficient distance away to suitably grow another apple tree. If the apple is not eaten, it may just sit there until it spoils. Even so, all is not lost, as the deteriorated apple will soften the ground where it rests and create a fertilized spot for the apple seeds to take root.

Such is the nature of the 9 cycle year. Like the fallen apple, it is a time of letting go and surrendering to the greater cycles of life. The apple gives up its material self and surrenders to life for the benefit of preparing the way for the next seeding cycle. This is a selfless, humanitarian act that comes from a sense of unconditional love for life over and above one's personal needs.

The first 7 months of the 9 year are a _review_ period, primarily of the 8 prior years and secondarily of all life to date. During this time, one's thoughts will constantly relive past events and a great deal of soul-searching will occur. People lost in your past will write or phone or appear out of the blue. This is a time to resolve outstanding issues and to forgive oneself and others for events and projects that went astray.

The last 5 months of the 9 year are a _preview_ of possible futures. Because the 9 year is a time of inspiration and insight, opportunities appear to be made in heaven. They look like perfection, just what you have waited for all of your life. During this period, it is most tempting to jump the gun and embrace the new opportunities. To do so is a great mistake. Simply observe and take notes during this time.

DO NOT MAKE MAJOR CHANGES IN A 9 CYCLE YEAR, PARTICULARLY DURING THE LAST 5 MONTHS OF THIS YEAR.

During a 9 year, the energy focuses in the 9th chakra, approximately 18 inches above the head. Because the energy focus is not in the body, the 9 year is one of extreme physical fatigue. This comes as a great shock after the invincible feeling of the 8 cycle year. A slight drop in physical energy will be noticeable in mid-December of the 8 year. Typically, people consider the slight drop of physical energy to be inconsequential and only temporary. The first 2 weeks of January are quite perky and then the 19th of January comes to pass. Within an hour, one feels exhausted, depleted, hollow, and empty. As if this isn't bad enough, the fatigue continues to increase daily, until July when one feels like a hollow eggshell attacking a cast iron frying pan. That's a silly image, but it always makes a lot of sense to anyone in July of a 9 cycle year. If you don't sit down or lie down every 4 hours during July, you will literally fall down.

I recommend scheduling the entire month of July as a holiday and a time of rest. It is not uncommon to sleep 12 to 14 hours or more during this period. If you force yourself to push on regardless of how you feel, you will undermine the seed that is critical to your well-being for the entire 9 years to come. Make sure you remember the importance of not physically pushing yourself in a 9 year. Living with exceptionally low energy for a period of 9 years is devastating. I've seen it happen.

It is especially important not to push yourself during July of a 9 cycle year.

People who are of particularly importance to you can enter or leave your life during a 9 cycle year. Leaving often includes death.

Do not be possessive in a 9 cycle year or loved ones will leave. Similarly, if you have a particular love for certain material possessions, the odds are very high that they will be lost or stolen in a 9 year.

The recommended strategy for a 9 year is:

- review life to date for the first 6 months
- take July off and rest as much as possible
- notice what ideas and opportunities present themselves in the last 5 months of the year.

Under no circumstances should you start new projects or begin intimate relationships regardless of how perfectly "made in heaven" they are — particularly during the last 5 months of the year. Grass will not grow in the fields of Alaska in December. The 9 cycle year is the winter of the 108 months of the overall cycle. This is a time to rest and contemplate what seeds you would most like to plant in June and July of your 1 cycle year.

A 9 year is a superb time for music, theatre, writing, and reading. Enjoy the inspiration and be gentle on your physical body.

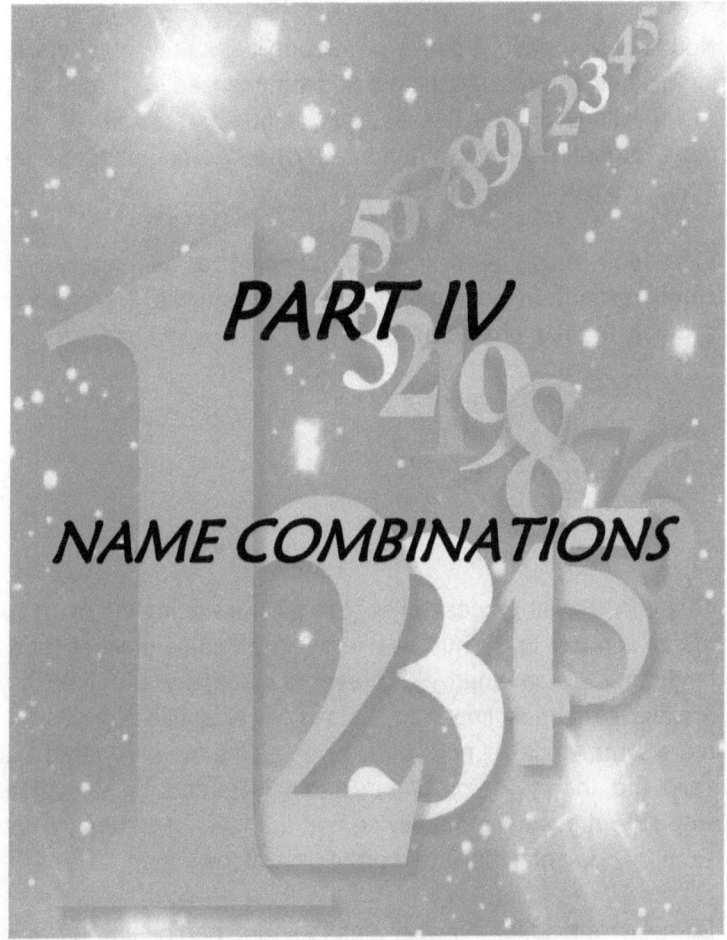

PART IV

NAME COMBINATIONS

CHAPTER 14 — COMPUTING NAME COMBINATIONS

NUMERIC VALUES OF THE LETTERS

Now that you have a sense of the qualities of the numbers as identified in the first 9 chapters and summarized in Chapters 10 & 11, let's apply the qualities of the numbers to names and discover just "what's in a name". As the following chapters will attest, it's plenty!!

First, you must learn how to compute a numeric, name combination from the numbers that are assigned to the letters or symbols of the alphabet as follows:

1	2	3	4	5	6	7	8	9
A	B	C	D	E	F	G	H	I
J	K	L	M	N	O	P	Q	R
S	T	U	V	W	X	Y	Z	

This very simple process of sequentially assigning the symbols of the alphabet to the numbers 1 to 9 is the same process for all languages of the world. The tests of symmetry and simplicity are two of the most important tests of any scientific theory — the more symmetrical, simple, and universal, the more valuable and valid the theory is for understanding life and the universe. Hopefully it goes without saying that the tests of symmetry and simplicity do not constitute a proof on their own merit.

Some of the letters of the alphabet are particularly easy to remember:

CLU	are all 3.	Threes love games and surprises and see life as a huge game of **CLUE**.
NEW	are all 5.	Fives thrive on **NEW**ness.
FOX	are all 6.	Sixes are noted for their intelligence and intuitive knowing like the **quick, smart FOX** in children's stories.

Here are some less obvious suggestions to help you remember the numeric values assigned to the alphabet:

JAS	are all 1.	**J**ocks, **A**thletics, & **S**ex
BTK	are all 2.	**B**onded **T**o **K**ids
VMD	are all 4.	**V**ery **M**eticulous **D**etail
GPY	are all 7.	**G**lorious **P**oetry **Y**earning
HQZ	are all 8.	**H**igh **Q**uality **Z**ebra or **H**uge, **Q**uality **Z**ebra
IR	are all 9.	**I**nspirational, **R**eligious or **I** a**R**e finished.

Create a set of images that work best for you to remember the numeric value of each letter. The helpful factor with the above suggestions is how the word groups relate to the qualities of the numbers that they represent. The fact that both business executives and zebras wear striped suits is a bit abstract, but it's a fun image and helps some people recall the numeric value of the letters HQZ. Use whatever system works for you.

THE NATURE OF WORDS

All words in the English language are made up of vowels and consonants. If there are no vowels in a "word", then the "word" is called an abbreviation. **Vowels are the heart and soul of a word.** Consonants are essentially fillers between the vowels similar to the unused keys between the notes that are played on the piano. Consonants are unquestionably important, but less important than vowels. It is the vowels that essentially give a word its life and tell us where the word is coming from, just as it is the heart of a person that truly tells us what their intention is.

COMPUTING NAME COMBINATIONS

In computing name combinations, the vowels are computed separately from the consonants. Special care must be taken when dealing with the letter "y". In numerology, the letter "y" is considered to be a vowel only if no other vowels exist in the word. For example, in the name Holly, "y" is a consonant, whereas, in the name Lynn, "y" is a vowel.

Using the numeric values assigned to the letters of the alphabet and keeping the vowels separate from the consonants, name combinations are computed as follows:

```
   6                6 = 6  sum of the vowels
J O H N
1     8 5   =      14 = 5  sum of the consonants
                   20 = 2  sum of vowels & consonants
```

When the sum of a series of letters exceeds 9, do one of the following procedures to reduce the numeric value to a single digit:

A. Repeatedly subtract 9 from the sum until the numeric value becomes 9 or less. Taking 24 as an example: 24 - 9 = 15, and 15 - 9 = 6. The desired number is 6.

or

B. Simply add the individual digits of the number together. Using the example of 24, the digits are 2 + 4 = 6.

Applying these rules to the numeric value computed for JOHN, notice that the sum of the consonants is 14 which reduces to 5 by either:

    A.   14 - 9 = 5
or
    B.   1 + 4 = 5

Pay particular attention to the following display of the name JOHN.

                6 **The source of John's thoughts, how he thinks**
J O H N   <u>5</u>
                2 **How John verbally expresses himself**

In this example, the sum of the consonants is a 5 and reflects the outer persona of the name. This factor is of such minor consequence in the overall scheme of analyzing names that I never reference it in personal consultations. On the other hand, I prefer to include it in name combinations because it confirms that the arithmetic of the computation is correct.

The sum of the vowels is called the **source number**. In the example of John, the source number of 6 reveals the source of his thoughts, where he is coming from, how he thinks, and what he would like to say. The sum of the vowels and consonants is called the **expression number**. In John's case, the expression number of 2 tells us how John verbally expresses himself. The critical question is, does John say what he would like to say? Is his mouth in gear with his mind? This is the single most important question to ask yourself whenever you are analyzing a name for its qualities.

What is the energy flow from the mind to the mouth? Does this person say what they think? Are the two factors in harmony or balance with each other?

The next 2 chapters are devoted to answering this question by reviewing 18 name combinations. Each example is composed of three parts:

Part A. What is the *"source number"* of this person's thinking pattern? What is their internal dialogue? Where are they coming from?

Part B. What is the *"expression number"*? What is their verbal style of expression?

Part C. What is the balance between their thoughts (Part A) and their verbal expression (Part B)? What is the energy flow from the mind to the mouth? Are they able to say what they think and feel?

In reference to **Part C**, "Are they able to say what they think?", one of three conditions will exist in all name combinations:

1. The verbal expression **restricts** the thoughts and holds them prisoners of their minds. In other words, the expression will suppress the mental process creating various levels of denying the internal dialogue. Restriction, suppression, and denial do not facilitate health or well-being.

2. The verbal expression **dissipates** the thought process and effectively dilutes the clarity of the mind, scattering ideas in all directions. As a result, valuable ideas are robbed of their depth.

3. The verbal expression **complements** the thought process and supports ideas in an atmosphere of balance. Ideas will be expressed with clarity, i.e., without restriction or dissipation.

The three key words to remember are:

RESTRICT	DISSIPATE	COMPLEMENT

CHAPTER 15 — NAMES WITH A 6 SOURCE NUMBER

This chapter summarizes all possible combinations beginning with a 6 source number: **6-4-1 6-5-2 6-6-3 6-7-4 6-8-5 6-9-6 6-1-7 6-2-8 6-3-9.** The emphasis is on the logic of how each expression number from 1 to 9 supports the source number of 6.

This chapter is not intended to be an exhaustive analysis of all the nuances that each combination embraces. Once you grasp the basic logic of analyzing a name combination, you will be able to extrapolate from the basics to whatever degree you desire.

EXAMPLE 1. As our first example, let's analyze John as defined by his name combination of 6-5-2.

Part A. John draws his mental energy from those qualities described by the 6 which are paternal, maternal, accountable, responsible, sensible, congenial, wholesome, and intelligent. Sound familiar?

Part B. John expresses the qualities of the 6 through the qualities of the 2 which are gentle, easygoing, gracious, sensitive, diplomatic, passive, and often quite procrastinating.

Part C. How does the 2 expression support the 6 source? The 2 softens the 6. Johns are very intelligent, capable, responsible people who are gracious and easygoing. They always have something pleasant to say about everybody and are perfect to choose for giving a toast to the bride or grace at the table. Their intelligence comes across in a smooth and friendly manner. They are excellent diplomats combining a superb depth of mind with finesse and tact. As delightful as they are to be with from a social standpoint, living or working with them can be another matter because, in the end (i.e. the expression number of 2), Johns have a very definite tendency to procrastinate and are well-known as "good old John" or "easygoing John".

Now it's time to make an important point. Each human being is a composite of many factors including at least: a first name, a surname, a destiny combination of the two names, a birthdate (which is discussed in Chapter 19), plus a cosmology inherited from both their parents and their social environment. In addition, there are often nicknames, maiden names, middle names, and sometimes several languages involved. This complex tapestry weaves an enormous variety of patterns affording each person their own uniqueness. Even so, there is always a common thread that is recognizable in every John that can be identified by analyzing his name. If John is an Aries, he will have a more forceful personality than a John who is a Taurus. Yet, within all Aries, John will be amongst the more congenial and gracious of his fellow Aries. Similarly, the personality of John will be recognizable whether John is a Harvard graduate running a multi-million dollar business or a street person dealing with surviving one day at a time.

EXAMPLE 2.   6-4-1   Cathie, Elsa, Eva, Faye, Kate, Lois, Mae, Stacey, Vera, Alfred, Bob, Bobby, Clifford, Edward, Frankie, Robb, Rod

Part A.   The source is the 6 which is the same as for John — paternal, maternal, accountable, responsible, sensible, congenial, wholesome, and intelligent.

Part B. The expression number is a 1 which is the male energy, the pioneer who is independent, self-sufficient, separate from, blunt, to the point, and calls a spade a spade and not a garden implement. The 1 is very honest and is not interested in diplomacy and tact.

Part C. How does the 1 expression support the 6 source? The 1 restricts the 6 creating a much more direct personality than is the nature of John. Bobs are people of few words in comparison to Johns. Corner a Bob and he will push back emotionally or physically whereas John will make every effort to graciously resolve a conflict before he will get physical. Most Johns will utterly refuse to resolve a conflict with physical force unless they have a preponderance of 1s in their other names and/or birthdate.

Here is another important point to remember. The 6 is wonderfully balanced in itself given its inherent qualities of being accountable, responsible, sensible, and wholesome. Consequently, the influence of any expression number on the 6 source is minimal. All other source numbers have a greater tendency to take on the negative aspects of their nature when they are combined with an expression number that does not support the source number. We will focus on this aspect after we complete the examples of the 6 source.

The first combination discussed in this chapter was 6-5-2 (John). Other names with the same combination as John are:

Dianne, Doris, Jade, Jamie, Nadine, Paige, Robyn, Tracie, Andrew, Charlie, Cody, Gerald, Jared, Morris, Tony

EXAMPLE 3. 6-6-3 Alice, Allie, Bobbi, Claire, Debra, Frances, Isabel, Jackie, Jane, Jean, Jessica, Madge, Maxine, Meghan, Charles, Ethan, James, Jock, Lyndon, Sean, Tom

Part A. The source is all the superb qualities of the 6.

Part B. The expression number is a 3 which is the extrovert, the entertainer, the child at play. The 3 is gregarious, cosmopolitan, cheerful, optimistic, magnetic, and imaginative. On the negative side, the 3 is argumentative, emotional, frivolous, and superficial.

Part C. How does the 3 expression support the 6 source? The 3 expression dissipates and scatters the energy of the 6 source. Toms, Jeans, Janes, etc. are all very capable, intelligent people who can be very hard to pin down. They love to quibble, tease, and generally argue the point. State what a beautiful clear day it is and they will likely take the opposite position to see if they can get a rise out of you. They are fun and playful but they truly can be a trial to those looking for commitments and decisions.

EXAMPLE 4. 6-7-4 Beverley, Hayley, Karen, Marcie, Melinda, Robin, Roslyn, Albert, Blake, Bradley, Dale, Fraser, Rory, Roy, Toni

Part A. The source number is a 6.

Part B. The expression number is a 4 which is the analyzer, the technician who is practical, patient, intellectual, reliable, disciplined, trustworthy, loyal, organized, and persevering. On the negative side, the 4 can be sceptical, narrow-minded, fussy, rigid, and stubborn.

Part C. How does the 4 expression support the 6 source? On one hand, the innate intelligence of the 6 is supported by the intellectual skills of the 4 creating an exceptionally capable analyzer who does not tend to get lost in the detail — an analyzer who actually knows when to quit. On the other hand, the 4 is not expressive and spontaneous. Dales and Karens are very capable people indeed. They tend to be on the reserved side, not favouring surprises or a lot of idle talk. The 4th physical sense is hearing. The 6-7-4 combination creates a superb listener who portrays a most sincere desire to understand other people's points of view. They have a non-threatening style of asking questions which combined with their ability to intelligently reflect on what they have heard, offers the other person a deep sense of being understood. They strive to understand and do not confuse their convictions with the opinions of others.

EXAMPLE 5. 6-8-5 Dolly, Eileen, Gayle, Janet, Jaye, Joy, Molly, Thelma, Bjorn, Clarke, Colt, Dave, Lloyd, Scott, Tommy, Wayne

Part A. The source number is a 6.

Part B. The expression number is a 5 which is the promoter who is very versatile, self-reliant, decisive, curious, enthusiastic, enterprising, freedom loving, adventurous, and insightful. This number thrives on newness. On the negative side, the 5 is critical, moody, temperamental, aggressive, impulsive, and intolerant.

Part C. How does the 5 expression support the 6 source? The 5 expression creates a very active 6 quality that is continually on the go. The impulsiveness of the 5 is held down to a dull roar by the 6 source creating a particularly vibrant quality that is intelligent and eager to participate in life.

Wayne Gretzky, the most renowned hockey player of all time, is a superb example of a 6-8-5 combination where the decisive, quick-moving qualities of the 5 are combined with all the sensible, intelligent qualities of the 6. Most people would prefer not to try to keep up with this combination, yet, as is always true with any combination beginning or ending with a 6, there is a keynote of sensibility infused in their character and a wholesomeness that is easy to admire.

EXAMPLE 6. 6-9-6 Cecilia, Diane, Edna, Flo, Helga, Janice, Kaye, Mabel Maggie, Marnie, Petra, Rae, Shelagh, Stella, Suzu, Kory, Alex, Dean, Don, Michael, Norm, Rolf, Troy, Victor, Wade

Part A. The source number is a 6.

Part B. The expression number is also a 6. This is our first example of a completely *balanced combination* and it is the only combination where the source number and the expression number are equal and the combination can be considered balanced.

Part C. Why is this combination considered to be balanced? First, the qualities of the source number of 6 are desirable in everyone's books — responsible, accountable, sensible, paternal, maternal, affectionate, artistic, stable, wise, congenial, and wholesome. Although the 6 has its negative side, it takes substantial forces to unhinge the 6 from its center of balance.

Secondly, the expression number of 6, which equals the source number, is all the same superb qualities, offering a clear channel of expression for the 6 source.

Sometimes, too much of a good thing can create the opposite effect and some 6-9-6s can be bossy, opinionated, faultfinding, and worriers. Often such an attitude stems from assuming too much responsibility for themselves and others. As a result, they can suffer from mental stress in the form of migraine headaches.

EXAMPLE 7. 6-1-7 Anne, Ashley, Gale, Glenda, Grace, Harriet, Hazel, Pearl, Darrell, Harvey, Marcel, Simon, Stewart, Walter, Warren

Part A. The source number is a 6.

Part B. The expression number is a 7 which is the introvert who is reflective, calm, refined, poised, dignified, philosophical, and inquisitive. On the negative side, the 7 is secretive, aloof, nervous, moody, and uncommunicative.

Part C. How does the 7 expression support the 6 source? Although the 7 restricts the verbal expression of the 6 and adds a tone of reservation and caution, the net result is a refined, poised, and dignified personality with all the positive qualities of the 6 and few of the negative qualities of the 7. They are exceptionally intelligent and capable people, although they keep a formal distance in personal relationships. They hold their body a bit on the stiff side and keep their head drawn back to signal it is inappropriate for anyone to stand too close. They play their cards very close to their chests and consider their personal affairs to be very private. It is difficult to really know someone with a 6-1-7 name. Their intelligence and dignity creates a strong cover personality that is initially hard to identify and is ultimately impenetrable.

EXAMPLE 8. 6-2-8 Bea, Brenda, Erika, Jasmine, Leah, Marge, Polly, Toby, Abe, Allen, Archie, Colin, Edgar, Floyd, Rob, Ross, Wallie

Part A. The source number is a 6.

Part B. The expression number is an 8 which is the

administrator who is just, confident, discriminating, shrewd, stable, ambitious, authoritative, and results-oriented. On the negative side, the 8 can be unscrupulous, materialistic, domineering, manipulative, and exploitive.

Part C. How does the 8 expression support the 6 source? This is a balanced combination because the 8 draws the energy of the 6 to a point of completion and fruition. Material success is typically substantial given that this combination begins with the capable, intelligent, responsible qualities of the 6. The discriminating and results oriented nature of the 8 doesn't add much humour or relaxation to the rather serious 6.

Although this is a **balanced combination,** it is not suitable for everyone. This is especially true for women because the external material focus of the 8 is at odds with the energy of the internal, female reproductive organs. Any combination beginning or ending in an 8 is not a desirable combination for a woman. The administrative and material gains that it fosters are typically offset with difficult menstrual cycles, inability to conceive, complications with childbirth, and often hysterectomies early in life (sometimes before 30 years of age).

EXAMPLE 9. 6-3-9   Angie, Carmen, Erica, Holly, Jody, Lori, Patrice, Sheila, Charley, Daniel, Earl, Gino, Harvie, Jake, Matthew, Ringo

Part A. The source number is a 6.

Part B. The expression number is a 9 which is the humanitarian who is generous, compassionate, empathic, and can express unconditional love and forgiveness. In addition, the 9 is intuitive, musical, artistic, and inspirational. On the negative side, the 9 can experience excessive self-pity, jealousy, and possessiveness.

Part C. How does the 9 expression support the 6 source? The 9 is in harmony with the 6 and offers a clear channel of expression for the 6 source. The 9 draws out the artistic, musical, and community-minded qualities of the 6 and adds a flair of inspiration to the personality. This combination can have its periods of being overly concerned with humanitarian projects and often gives too much of itself. Such periods do not last long as the good old sensible 6 will come to its senses and maintain an atmosphere of responsibility. Similarly, the 6-3-9 can have intense moments of jealousy, temper, and possessiveness which pass rather quickly.

CHAPTER 16 — NAMES WITH A 6 EXPRESSION NUMBER

This chapter summarizes all possible combinations ending with a 6 expression number. The emphasis is on the logic of how each source number from 1 to 9 is supported by the expression number of 6. This chapter is a mirror image of Chapter 15. **Part D** has been added to the description of each name combination to compare it to its mirror image.

Chapter 15:
6-4-1 6-5-2 6-6-3 6-7-4 6-8-5 6-9-6 6-1-7 6-2-8 6-3-9

Chapter 16:
1-5-6 2-4-6 3-3-6 4-2-6 5-1-6 6-9-6 7-8-6 8-7-6 9-6-6

In Chapter 15, each expression number of 1 to 9 modified the 6 source number to some degree. Although the stability of the 6 was apparent in the analysis of each combination, the expression number restricted, dissipated, or complemented the 6 source number.

In Chapter 16, we will see how the 6 expression number always supports the source number in a positive manner, adding a note of sensibility and reasonability to the source numbers of 1 to 9.

Again, the descriptions will focus on the logic and will not be an exhaustive analysis of each name combination.

EXAMPLE 1. 1-5-6 Dawn, Fayth, Irene, Lesley, Lillian, Lydia, Sally, Traci, Bryan, Chester, Gary, Grant, Ian, Reggie, Sam, Stephen

Part A. The source number is a 1 which is the male energy, the pioneer who is independent, self-sufficient, separate from, blunt, and to the point. The 1 is very honest and is not interested in diplomacy and tact.

Part B. The expression number is a 6 which is the counsellor who is paternal, maternal, accountable, responsible, sensible, congenial, wholesome, and intelligent.

Part C. How does the 6 expression support the 1 source? Although this combination can be very self-centered, headstrong, and independent, they always return to an atmosphere of sensibility. Primarily, they look out first for themselves, and second, they keep an eye on the needs of their family. This combination creates a strong willed individual who knows what they want and goes straight after their desires. Women with this combination are competitive and do not take a back seat to their mates at any time.

Part D. How does the 1-5-6 differ from the 6-4-1? The key difference lies in the source number of 1 versus 6. The 1 source number is more head strong, independent, and self-sufficient than the 6 source number which is attuned to paternal, maternal, and community-minded attitudes. The 6-4-1 combination can be blunt and to the point, yet they draw from a more conceptual basis than the 1-5-6 combination, which draws strongly from the physical senses and pioneering instincts.

EXAMPLE 2.   2-4-6   Alisa, Ava, Connie, Leanne, Lonnie, Maria, Marsha, Matilda, Devon, Fabian, Hector, Isaac, Joel, Robbie, Robert, Verdon

Part A.   The source number is a 2 which is the diplomat and mediator who is tactful, intuitive, sensitive, persuasive, cooperative, considerate, adaptable, responsive, and nurturing.

Part B.   The expression number is a 6.

Part C.   How does the 6 expression number support the 2 source? This is a delightful, warm, loving combination that will always go the extra mile to seek understanding. At the same time, they can graciously say no when required and do not betray themselves as other combinations do which are strong in the 2 quality. Nor are they prone to procrastinating which is a typical weakness of the 2. They are clear, calm, centered, a delight to be with and always find something loving and supportive to say about everyone.

Part D.   How does the 2-4-6 differ from the 6-5-2? Although the 2-4-6 has a gentle nature, they follow through to completion on a consistent basis. The 6-5-2 is more intelligent and has greater depth than the 2-4-6, but they are very prone to procrastinating and, in the end, they water down their efforts and don't complete what they start. Consequently, the 2-4-6 will often achieve more than the 6-5-2 even though the 6-5-2 has greater depth and insight.

EXAMPLE 3.   3-3-6   Dorothy, Jollean, Judy, Maryanna, Rosemary, Suki, Veronica, Cameron, Dunc, Dustin, Jaromey, Leonard, Norton, Ryun, Stu

Part A.   The source number is a 3 which is the extrovert, the entertainer who is magnetic, musical, cheerful, optimistic, gregarious, cosmopolitan, articulate, imaginative, and generous.

Part B. The expression number is a 6.

Part C. This is our third example of a completely **balanced name.** Why is a 3-3-6 combination considered balanced when the 1-5-6 and the 2-4-6 are not? The 1-5-6 and the 2-4-6 are respectably wholesome combinations. Yet, the 3-3-6 outshines them because the 3 is a composite of the better qualities of the 1 and the 2. i.e. the bonding of the 1 (male energy) and the 2 (female energy) gives birth to the 3.

The accountable and responsible instincts of the 6 draw out the positive aspects of the 3 and create a particularly congenial and wholesome personality. People with this combination have a superb sense of humour. At the same time, they are very clear on their direction and goals in all areas of life. They prefer to do business in an easygoing manner but they do not hesitate to back up their smile with the power of the 1.

Part D. How does the 3-3-6 differ from the 6-6-3? In the end, the 3-3-6 will take their projects to completion, whereas the 6-6-3 will dissipate their efforts and scatter their energies to the four winds. The 6-6-3 combination is marvellously capable and, at the same time, it can be exasperating to watch them waste their potential.

EXAMPLE 4. 4-2-6 Audry, Faun, Joenna, Lurleen, Roseanna, Ruthann, Uta, Arthur, Audy, Barnaum, Dagwood, Murray, Raymund, Truman

Part A. The source number is a 4 which is the technician, the analyzer who is practical, patient, intellectual, reliable, disciplined, honest, punctual, loyal, organized, and persevering. They can be sceptical, fussy, rigid, dogmatic, and dull.

Part B. The expression number is a 6.

Part C. How does the 6 expression number support the 4 source? The 6 expression number helps to draw out any number with which it is associated. The 6 is a blessing in this case because the 4 is reserved and not very outgoing by nature. Even with the help of the 6 expression, this combination is not very vibrant or outgoing. They are serious about their work and take great pride in being organized, and efficient. This combination creates exceptionally good analyzers who can communicate their insights with clarity and precision. The 4 is about education and the 6 reflects accountability and responsibility. Consequently, those with a 4-2-6 combination are excellent teachers.

Part D. How does the 4-2-6 differ from the 6-7-4? The difference in this example is subtle indeed, given the similarity in nature of the 4 and the 6 who both love to stay at home and are reserved by nature. The basic difference is in the energy flow from the source to the expression number. The 4-2-6 starts from an analytical attitude and moves to completion through the 6 expression. The 6-7-4 starts from a conceptual, intellectual space and moves into analysis. The end result for the 6-7-4 is to get lost in the detail and become stuck whereas the 4-2-6 will move out of the detail into the awareness of the 6.

EXAMPLE 5. 5-1-6 Christine, Ginger, Kristine, Paula, Peggy, Jeri, Shirley, Benny, Clive, Erwin, Fred, Herb, Kenny, Timmie, Vincent

Part A. The source number is a 5 which is about rapid growth, change, travel, decisiveness, enthusiasm, adventure, insight, enterprising, promotion, and freedom.

Part B. The expression number is a 6.

Why Do Numbers Count

Part C. This is a vibrant, alive and a dynamic combination. No moss grows under the feet of the 5 who has outstanding analytical skills and a determination to move forward at every opportunity. The 6 expression number offers a clear channel for the aliveness of the 5. The 6 helps to stabilize the 5 by adding an air of caution, responsibility, and accountability. Internally, these people are very intense. Externally, they are congenial and progressive. This combination demands freedom and a partner who can live with their intensity. They exude a great deal of confidence and trust in their lightning fast mental abilities. They have no fear of getting backed into a corner or of being taken advantage of in any way, at any time.

Part D. How does the 5-1-6 differ from the 6-8-5? Internally, the 5-1-6 is more intense than the 6-8-5. The 6-8-5 is more relaxed and is in less of a hurry, although not by much. The 5-1-6 is a healthier combination than the 6-8-5 because the end result of the 5-1-6 combination is a 6 which reflects the qualities of accountability and responsibility. The end result of the 6-8-5 combination is the 5 which tends to attract bitter experiences because of its impatient, intolerant, and impulsive nature. Mind you, such negative qualities of the 5 have a hard time manifesting when the 5 is in relationship to the 6, as it is in the 6-8-5 combination.

EXAMPLE 6.   6-9-6   Cecilia, Diane, Edna, Flo, Helga, Janice, Kaye, Mabel, Maggie, Marnie, Petra, Rae, Shelagh, Stella, Suzu, Kory, Alex, Dean, Don, Michael, Norm, Rolf, Tory, Victor, Wade

Part A. The source number is a 6.

Part B. The expression number is also a 6. This is our first example of a completely *balanced combination* and is the only combination where the source number and the expression number are equal and the combination can be considered balanced.

Part C. Why is this combination considered to be balanced? First, the qualities of the source number of 6 are desirable in everyone's books — responsible, accountable, sensible, paternal, maternal, affectionate, artistic, stable, wise, congenial, and wholesome. Although the 6 has its negative side, it takes substantial forces to unhinge the 6 from its center of balance.

Second, the expression number of 6 which equals the source number, is all the same superb qualities, offering a clear channel of expression for the 6 source.

Sometimes, too much of a good thing can create the opposite effect and some 6-9-6's can be bossy, opinionated, faultfinding, worriers. Often such an attitude stems from assuming too much responsibility for themselves and others. As a result, they can suffer from mental stress in the form of migraine headaches.

EXAMPLE 7. 7-8-6 Lenore, Lisa-Marie, Lorna, Mary-Jane, Phoebe, Rhonda, Geoffrey, Harmon, Howard, Lyn, Malcolm, Mallory, Somerset

Part A. The source number is a 7 which is the poet and the philosopher who is introspective, inquisitive, reflective, calm, refined, poised, dignified, insightful, spiritually attuned, and mystical.

Part B. The expression number is a 6.

Part C. This is a dignified and refined combination that draws from an abstract mental context. They are capable of capturing concepts which go beyond words and formulating concrete ideas around their rarefied insights. They are exceptionally intuitive about what is happening behind the scenes — to what is not being said that should be said.

Part D. How does the 7-8-6 differ from the 6-1-7? Although the 7-8-6 combination lives in an internal realm of abstractions, they strive to remain in contact with family, friends, and the outside world. In contrast, although the 6-1-7's heart is deeply bonded with family and friends, they draw back and keep a formal distance between themselves and others. The difference lies with the placement of the 7. The expression number always reflects the end result of the combination. The 7 expression number withdraws and takes on some of the less desirable qualities of the 7 such as being secretive, repressed, aloof, nervous, and moody on occasion.

EXAMPLE 8. 8-7-6 Antoinette, Morgana, Muriel, Pandora, Roxanna, Susen, Boone, Dustie, Humphrey, Huntley, Purcell, Roben, Tucker

Part A. The source number is an 8 which is the administrator who is confident, discriminating, shrewd, ambitious, authoritative, thorough, efficient, results-oriented, and materialistic.

Part B. The expression number is a 6.

Part C. This combination has a keen business sense with a strong focus on home and family. They desire an expensive home with all the trimmings. Home life would be well organized, if not regimented. This is a no nonsense combination with a keen eye for results. These people take life rather seriously.

Part D. How does the 8-7-6 differ from the 6-2-8? The 6-2-8 is a more desirable combination because the energy moves from the exceptionally competent 6 to the results-oriented and fruition qualities of the 8. The 6-2-8 works toward a successful completion, whereas the 8-7-6 can be predisposed with success and lack a certain patience in gaining their due rewards. In other words, the 8-7-6 can be smug and pompous in comparison to the 6-2-8 and not as willing to allow life to unfold naturally.

EXAMPLE 9. 9-6-6 Claudine, Ginny, Kim, Laurel, Lil, Pauline, Tilly, Trixy, Billy, Britt, Dirk, Griffin, Hugo, Skipy, Tim, Vik

Part A. The source number is a 9 which is the humanitarian who is forgiving, generous, compassionate, empathic, tolerant, intuitive, musical, artistic, visionary, and inspirational.

Part B. The expression number is a 6.

Part C. All the qualities of the 9 are desirable and wonderful when they can be realized, which only happens when a 6 is in combination with the 9. This is a delightful combination which is full of love, understanding, insight, and an ability to interact with friends, family, and community. It is one of the better combinations available. IBM is a 9-6-6 combination which reflects clearly in their corporate character.

Part D. How does the 9-6-6 differ from the 6-3-9? Beginning a combination with a 9 is much more desirable than ending a combination with a 9. Why? The 9-6-6 combination brings the inspired ideals of unconditional love into the practical, accountable, responsible, and sensible realm of the 6. The 6-3-9 combination expands the basic accountable and responsible nature of the 6 into the inspired ideals of the 9 including the keynotes of forgiveness, letting go, and surrender. Although these qualities are spiritually desirable, the 9 quality tends to experience its fair share of material and emotional losses. Fortunately, the 6 source in the 6-3-9 combination helps mitigate the material and emotional losses of the 9 expression number. The 6-3-9 is a bit flamboyant for a first name, yet makes an excellent surname as discussed in Chapter 23. In comparison, the 9-6-6 is most desirable first name.

CHAPTER 17 — ALL POSSIBLE NAME COMBINATIONS

The following table lists all possible name combinations (81). So far, we have considered the logic of the 17 combinations that are shaded. I recommend that you read about half this chapter. Skip about and read the ones that catch your eye, or review only the combinations in bold. Carry on with the rest of the book when the logic of name combinations becomes comfortable to you.

1-9-1 1-1-2 1-2-3 1-3-4 1-4-5 1-5-6 **1-6-7 1-7-8 1-8-9**

2-8-1 **2-9-2 2-1-3 2-2-4 2-3-5 2-4-6** 2-5-7 2-6-8 2-7-9

3-7-1 3-8-2 3-9-3 3-1-4 3-2-5 **3-3-6 3-4-7 3-5-8** 3-6-9

4-6-1 4-7-2 4-8-3 4-9-4 4-1-5 **4-2-6** 4-3-7 4-4-8 **4-5-9**

5-5-1 5-6-2 5-7-3 5-8-4 5-9-5 **5-1-6 5-2-7 5-3-8 5-4-9**

6-4-1 6-5-2 6-6-3 6-7-4 6-8-5 6-9-6 6-1-7 6-2-8 6-3-9

7-3-1 **7-4-2 7-5-3** 7-6-4 7-7-5 **7-8-6 7-9-7 7-1-8** 7-2-9

8-2-1 8-3-2 8-4-3 **8-5-4** 8-6-5 **8-7-6** 8-8-7 **8-9-8** 8-1-9

9-1-1 9-2-2 9-3-3 9-4-4 9-5-5 **9-6-6** 9-7-7 **9-8-8** 9-9-9

The 17 combinations from the previous two chapters have been repeated here to offer all 81 combinations in sequence as a reference guide for your future convenience.

In this chapter, each combination is overviewed without repeating the key words and dividing the discussion into parts A,

B, C, & D. Even so, keep in mind that the insights offered for the following combinations have been arrived at by asking the question: *how does the expression number support the source number — does the expression number **restrict, dissipate, or complement** the source number?*

Once again, be aware that each of the following combinations add or subtract from the overall potential and general character of each individual who uses a specific combination in his or her life. When you read that John is this way and that way, remember that the name John reflects certain qualities, yet the human being named John *is much more than one specific name.* Even so, each name that used has a dramatic impact on one's character and life's experience.

COMBINATIONS WITH A SOURCE NUMBER OF 1

No individual is simply one name or all of their names, although each name used will influence the overall personality and life experience as follows:

EXAMPLE 1.   1-9-1   Brittany, Hilary, Kay, Kimberley, Mavis, Patty, Sherrie, Barry, Dan, Ivan, Pat, Peter, Ralph, Verne, Wally, Ward

Although this combination is comprised of pure male energy, it should not be confused with the label of egocentric, macho, and chauvinistic which are out of balance, discordant qualities of the 1. These people exhibit all the typical 1 qualities of being strong willed, independent, and self-sufficient. Their physical and emotional needs are basic and uncomplicated. They seldom have mood swings and are very much the same nature day in and day out. They are candid with others and appreciate the same in return. They avoid a lot of social activity and have few friends. Although they are slow to make friends, once they do, they make friends for life. On the other hand, if they ever terminate a friendship, it's under exceptional and extreme circumstances and they will never reconsider their decision. They enjoy hard, physical work and can be very good with their hands. When accidents occur, their leadership skills come to the fore and they instinctively take charge and pragmatically do whatever has to be done without hesitation. Otherwise, they prefer to work on their own and avoid the public eye.

Women using this combination virtually, always wear pants — skirts and dresses feel foreign to them. Both men and women with these numbers dress simply and like strong, solid colours. The 1 quality has basic material needs as described by the metaphor of the pioneer. In comparison, the 1-7-8 combination is much more prone to being materialistic and egocentric because the 8 expression focuses on external, material form.

EXAMPLE 2. 1-1-2 Ann, April, Candy, Denise, Evelyn, Gail, Kathy, Marilyn, Cary, Craig, Dylan, Hart, Joshua, Larry, Max, Walt, Zach

The cliche for this combination is "their bark is worse than their bite". The 1 source has very strong opinions and is not interested in diplomacy and tact. In contrast, the 2 expression is all about diplomacy and tact. Imagine a 1-1-2 telling a friend about how angry they are with their partner. "When I see that so-and-so again, I'm going to tell them in no uncertain terms just what I think. They'll never push me around again. Boy, am I ever going to give them a piece of my mind." At this moment, in walks the person in question, and the 1-1-2 says, "Oh **HI HONEY**, I was just talking about you. How are you? Are you having a nice day?" The bark was worse than the bite — lots of talk, but typically no action.

Although the 2 expression softens the 1 and offers some social skills and a sense of connection to other people, the 1 and the 2 are opposite in nature and a sense of confusion surrounds most of their activities. They can never quite decide which foot to stand on from one moment to the next. Consequently, they have difficulty achieving their goals and can appear to be shallow minded.

EXAMPLE 3. 1-2-3 Cathy, Ellen, Esther, Liza, Marg, Mary, Nancy, Pam, Rita, Art, Delbert, Hal, Jeffrey, Lanny, Lindsay, Martin, Wendell

This is a very pleasant combination that works particularly well for women even though it begins with a 1 source number which is basic, male energy. For a woman, it fosters a definite sense of independence and strength that isn't overly masculine because the 3 expression embraces a well defined balance of feminine and masculine qualities. This combination allows people to be their own person, yet they have a cosmopolitan and gregarious personality. For the most part, they are generous, cheerful, self-contained, and consistent in their character. Surprisingly though, when they get backed into a corner, they will physically punch their contender. Why? Because the physical, independent 1 is living under the cover of the pleasant and bouncy 3 expression. Their weakness lies in scattering their efforts and in not completing what they start. They are pioneers at heart with good verbal skills. They can be compulsive eaters craving too many heavy, starchy foods.

EXAMPLE 4. 1-3-4 Daisy, Gina, Kaitlin, Kathi, Linda, Michelle, Tracy, Wilma, Al, Danny, David, Dexter, Gene, Herbert, Lee, Ryan, Steven

The cliche for these people is *"I'm from Missouri — don't tell me, show me"*. The independent, self-sufficient, persevering, practical qualities of the 1 find little relief with the analytical, intellectual, dogmatic, stubborn, dull, and plodding qualities of the 4 expression number. These individuals have to know how things work in a tangible, practical, physical sense. As children, they take everything apart to see how it works. Many accountants and lawyers are 1-3-4's. They simply don't move until they are ready to move. They can be very thick-headed. Over a lifetime, they can accumulate a respectable estate, not out of sensitivity and responsiveness to life, but because they simply have no comprehension of when it is time to quit.

Davids are often called Dave which is a 6-8-5 combination.

Whichever name is used the most frequently has the greatest impact on their personality. In comparison to David, the name Dave is exceptionally bright, insightful, and decisive. Dave functions on intuition and is impatient, not wanting to wade through endless facts. In this sense, the quick minded, decisive nature of Dave can work as a helpful complement to the obstinate nature of David.

The important point to remember here is that Davids are not your typical 1-3-4 combination if he also uses the name Dave.

EXAMPLE 5. 1-4-5 Barb, Dee, Ethel, Fay, Gladys, Lisa, Shelley, Vivian, Bart, Clay, Frank, Lars, Lennie, Marty, Marvin, Zack

The name Frank speaks clearly for this combination which is just that, "very frank", to the point, "no muss, no fuss". The numbers 1 and 5 are similar in nature — independent, self-sufficient, determined, and initiating. They are very much their own person and will not tolerate interference in any form. The 5 expression adds an abundance of vitality to the 1 source creating a whirlwind of energy. This is not a talkative combination, but they have little trouble speaking their mind in a very blunt, critical manner. These people make great travelling salesmen where they can be on-the-go, free, independent, and promotional. They have no qualms about using high pressure tactics. Home is not where their heart lives.

EXAMPLE 6. 1-5-6 Dawn, Fayth, Irene, Lesley, Lillian, Lydia, Sally, Traci, Bryan, Chester, Gary, Grant, Ian, Reggie, Sam, Stephen

Although this combination can be very self-centered, headstrong, and independent, they always return to an atmosphere of sensibility and congeniality. Primarily, they look out first for themselves and second, they keep an eye on the needs of their family. This combination creates a strong willed individual who knows what they want and goes straight after their desires. Their nature lends itself to being good bosses in the sense that they uphold firm convictions and are not upset by the emotional needs of others. Although they are very much their own person, they are sufficiently receptive to new ideas that others see them as being reasonable and trustworthy. These people can be very creative in a practical sense. Women with this combination are competitive and do not take a back seat to their mates at any time. These numbers are in the top 20% of the best combinations.

EXAMPLE 7.   1-6-7   Bette, Clair, Ellie, Hilda, Jan, Kathryn, Sylvia, Yvette, Brad, Carl, Derek, Hank, Harry, Jack, Mark, Richard

The cliché for these numbers is "take it or leave it". Why? The 1 source number, which speaks directly and to the point, finds expression through the 7 which is introverted and avoids talking. When the 1 and 7 are combined, there is neither a desire nor an outlet for verbal expression, hence a personality that is reserved and not open to much discussion. These people have a way of quietly saying "no" that is so absolute and final that any further discussion would be futile. The 7 always adds a sense of dignity to any combination as it does with the 1-6-7 offering at least a limited air of grace to their rough and ready, pioneering nature. These names foster a very self-contained, private demeanour that can prefer to live on their own. They often put forward an assertive, positive personality as a cover up for their sensitivities. Misunderstandings and confrontation are not strangers to them.

Why Do Numbers Count

EXAMPLE 8. 1-7-8 Beckie, Cynthia, Fawn, Helen, Leslie, Mila, Val, Virginia, Brian, Gavin, Mac, Nat, Pierre, Randy, Ray, Sammy, Steve

This combination is interested in results — practical, tangible, physical, demonstrable results. They are not interested in stories or excuses. They operate their lives like a steamroller. If it doesn't work, get a bigger hammer. Their predisposition with material success creates an ambience of "I want what I want, and I want it now, thank you very much." Tact and patience are not among their strong points. They are self-starters, well organized, and have leadership skills.

If this combination gets lost in materiality, they can be the most ego-centric, macho combination of all because the negative side of the 8 is power-hungry, unscrupulous, domineering, oppressive, manipulative, and exploitive.

This is a most undesirable combination for a woman. If there are not offsetting qualities in other names, a woman with this combination is well described as a man in a woman's body. Women with these numbers are very prone to all manner of reproductive system disorders. It is not uncommon for them to have hysterectomies before they are 30 years of age. In addition, sexual intimacy can be extraordinary difficult for women with these numbers. Why is this so? The source number is a 1 which is male energy and the 8 is focused on material externals which is in contradiction to the internal nature of female sexuality.

Even though males with this combination have an exceptionally strong sexual focus, they seldom manifest generative disorders. They are completely preoccupied with money, sex, and power and have little or no understanding of personal intimacy.

EXAMPLE 9. 1-8-9 Debbie, Dinah, Jennifer, Miriam, Patsy, Sandy, Tammy, Clark, Clement, Eddie, Ernest, Garth, Jay, Matt, Stan

The 9 expression is the complete opposite of the 1 source and creates a tremendous internal polarity which results in confusion and an explosive nature. The 1 source appears to be stable and dependable, yet with little warning these people can succumb to fits of anger and emotional outbursts that are very intense and unpleasant. This tendency can be well camouflaged by the inspirational, humanitarian 9 for some time but the two opposites can only survive for so long before they come unglued. This combination can suffer from nervous disorders later in life.

A 9 expression number typically depletes whatever source number it is with. Only the 6 source number survives well with a 9 expression as denoted by the 6-3-9 combination in example 54.

Why Do Numbers Count

COMBINATIONS WITH A SOURCE NUMBER OF 2

No individual is simply one name or all of their names, although each name used will influence the overall personality and life experience as follows:

EXAMPLE 10. 2-8-1 Arlene, Elaine, Hannah, Lana, Noel, Rebecca, Sabrina, Zoe, Adam, Alan, Joey, Joseph, Leon, Lorne, Scottie, Sherlock

In this example, the desire is for peace and harmony, yet circumstances constantly dictate the need to confront issues. When these people are under pressure they tend to blurt out things which they had promised themselves not to say. Their direct manner in such situations is distressing to their desire for congenial relationships. They like knowing the details of personal confidences, but when faced with a direct question, they are compelled to tell the truth. They have a gentle heart and a direct manner of speaking. Often they feel much more than they express.

EXAMPLE 11. 2-9-2 Catherine, Diana, Heather, Marian, Melody, Sarah, Violet, Adrian, Benoit, Dana, Desmond, Forrest, Foster, Rolfe

No other combination is purer in feminine energies than the 2-9-2. Where the 1 is all about establishing boundaries, the 2 is all about removing boundaries and bonding. No one is more concerned with diplomacy, tact, and cooperation. Unfortunately, too much focus in one area of life creates an imbalance. These people are often known as *shrinking Violets* who avoid any and all issues at any cost. The price they pay for peace is a denial of their own personal needs resulting in a passive, impractical, indecisive, and fearful personality. In earlier years, this combination may try to compensate for their inner experience by putting on a good front, a strong offensive. Unfortunately, the less positive side will prevail in the long run. To maintain a healthy, vibrant life, this combination needs to learn how to effectively negotiate and not give themselves away. If they have integrated a sense of self-respect, their intuitive, responsive, and nurturing instincts can generate a most persuasive personality, indeed.

This combination can be impossible to pin down. They can have a slippery personality that can spontaneously concoct the most frivolous, clever, unrelated excuses imaginable. When you back them into a corner to solicit a direct answer, they can be as flabbergasted at what they say as you are. They are masters at "little white lies". Only if you have an abundance of 2 in your nature, will you understand that saying "no" physically hurts !!

The predominance of 2 in this example results in poor circulation creating a physiology vulnerable to cold weather. This combination suffers from "cold feet" both physically and psychologically. They readily retain body fluids and are prone to being overweight. They are subject to kidney trouble and weak bladders.

These people have very quick, receptive minds. Their greatest enigma is forgetting just as quickly as they learn — particularly material facts and people's names. Forgetting people's names is devastating to them because their entire sense of diplomacy and tact centers around being personal with people. Often their mind will go blank in the midst of making personal introductions to their oldest friends.

Possibly the most classic 2-9-2 name is Cinderella.

Why Do Numbers Count

EXAMPLE 12. 2-1-3 Anna, Charlene, Dollie, Jocelyn, Mollie, Rose, Sandra, Corey, Elliott, Geoff, Graham, Joe, Leroy, Ronie, Tommie

In comparison with the 2-9-2, this combination has some of the spunk of the 3 which is helpful only to a small degree. Unfortunately, the 3 expression number scatters the energy of the passive 2 and creates a combination which is very laid-back and amongst the world's great procrastinators. These people love to talk and they seem to have all day to say absolutely nothing. Imagine talking to a "good ol' Joe, easygoing Joe" and in his slow drawl he says, "Hi, how is it going? How you been lately? Garsh, darn but it's good to see you. Oh sure, I have things to do, but tell me how you are doing first." This combination typically is so "wishy-washy" and has so little substance to their personality that well-known Joes are often referred to as "Joe who?". They love to gossip and can be very graceful liars.

This combination has a very strong tendency to put on weight for a number of reasons. For one, the 2 quality dislikes saying "no" and the impulsive 3 quality adores food. That's double trouble right there. In addition, the easygoing, laid-back 2 is unwilling to exercise. They are fond of sugars and appease their emotional desires by constantly snacking.

EXAMPLE 13. 2-2-4 Jeannie, Joyce, Kathleen, Martina, Nicole, Theresa, Allan, Christopher, Gordie, Monte, Morey, Nathan, Rodger

The easygoing 2 wants to resolve issues and remove the boundaries that separate people from one another. On the other hand, the 4 expression is completely caught in definitions and material form. The result is confusion and mental anguish between trying to dissolve boundaries while at the same time striving to establish more definition.

The passive 2 and the slow-to-decide 4 fosters a personality that is mentally slow and has very poor concentration. The 2 is interested in the emotional climate whereas the 4 is compelled to talk only of the facts of the situation. The result is a very fussy quality that is slow to change and forever lives in a great deal of emotional turmoil, personal slights, and misunderstandings. This combination is not known for their depth of mind.

The 4 is a collector and hates to let go of anything. Consequently, it creates a withholding nature, a quality of being constipated. Any combination ending in a 4 will be prone to having large hips, buttocks, and elimination problems.

The name Allen is a 6-2-8 which is a very different set of qualities from Allan. See Example 53.

EXAMPLE 14.   2-3-5   Abigail, Bonnie, Darlene, Lara, Melanie, Patricia, Yvonne, Boyce, Dewayne, Earle, Errol, Gregory, Leo, Wellington

In this case, the easygoing, peace loving 2 finds expression through the knife-edge, assertive, promotional, and independent 5. This doesn't work well at all because the expression number is in sharp contrast to the source number. This combination is highly sensitive, intense, and discordant.

These people suffer not only from a lot of *external* tension, but also from a great deal of *internal* tension because they can seldom graciously express what they are feeling inside. They can make a tremendous effort to be gracious and understanding, yet they simply can't leave well enough alone and insist on having the last word. No matter how hard they try to cover up their deep emotions, their expression has a sharp bite to it. As a result, their life is full of bitter experiences and misunderstandings which truly distresses their gentle inner self. Essentially, they have little control over what they say. They can suffer from intense stomach pains and from a great deal of "heart ache". This is not a healthy or a stable combination.

EXAMPLE 15.   2-4-6   Alisa, Ava, Connie, Leanne, Lonnie, Maria, Marsha, Matilda, Devon, Fabian, Hector, Isaac, Joel, Robbie, Robert, Verdon

This is a delightful, gracious, warm, loving combination that will always go the extra mile to seek understanding. At the same time, they will not give themselves away with excessive procrastination or an inability to say no. They are a delight to be with and always find something loving and supportive to say about everyone. Their compassionate and tactful nature embraces both practical and artistic skills. They have a strong love for home and family and can also do well in the business world.

This is a desirable combination for a woman because the 2 source number is in tune with her instinctual nature. On the other hand, males using this combination can be very gentle, if not passive. Robert is often called Bob which is a 6-4-1 and affords Robert a strong measure of male energy.

EXAMPLE 16.   2-5-7   Adrienne, Annette, Elizabeth, Martha, Tanya, Vanna, Wanda, Donnie, Georg, Gregor, Morley, Nelson, Nero, Vernon, Wolfe

This is one of the most sensitive of all the combinations because both the source and the expression numbers are gentle and vulnerable. The nurturing, loving nature of the 2 which thrives on relationships is thwarted by the 7 which prefers a great deal of privacy and alone time. The 7 isolates the 2 from the rest of the world. The result is a loving, gentle heart that never finds fulfilment. This combination finds it difficult to communicate their deep emotions and suffers from an unreasonable number of misunderstandings. Although they appear calm and refined, they are moody, jealous, easily hurt, very idealistic, and have little or no self-confidence. They can be very passive and do not like to work at anything. The extreme emotional sensitivity of this combination will reflect in poor health including very delicate lungs and weak hearts. They function on a very low level of physical energy and require a great deal of extra sleep. They take a very long time to wake-up and are definitely not morning people. These people dress with an elegant flair and can be very attractive physically.

EXAMPLE 17.   2-6-8   Carla, Chelsea, Clara, Cleo, Danielle, Jeane, Roxie, Bobbie, Brodie, Cole, Godfrey, Leeland, Randall, Trevor

The 2-4-6 and the 2-6-8 are similar in many ways. Both are very considerate, loving, and affectionate, yet they know how to stand their ground and not give themselves away. This is a very charming personality that can do exceptionally well as a mediator or a diplomat. The 2-6-8 is much more materially oriented than is the 2-4-6 and favours business over home and family life. Like the 2-4-6, the 2-6-8 combination is very gentle for a male. These people desire quality and quantity but are short on the ambition required for the fulfilment of their dreams. They frequently fantasize about winning the lottery or inheriting money.

Although this combination creates a very pleasant ambience for a female, it is not a good combination for a woman from a health standpoint. The source number of 2 which is directly related to feminine energy is in contradiction to the 8 which is externally oriented. The contrast can manifest in reproductive system disorders.

EXAMPLE 18. 2-7-9 Anita, Jaylene, Marcia, Marlee, Olive, Sophie, Valerie, Barnaby, Holmes, Lawrence, Ogden, Ozzie, Rodney, Roger

This is an exceptionally loving, gentle, and affectionate quality. This combination totally thrives on love, attention, acknowledgement, cuddling, and sharing everything they do with someone else. Their humanitarian ideas are exceptionally high and they seek peace at all costs, which can work to their detriment. These people can have a terrible time saying no to anyone. They have an extremely soft heart and will typically give their last dollar to a pan-handler. This combination easily becomes enmeshed in relationships where they completely lose themselves within the relationship. They are idealistic dreamers and can be deeply religious. Their emotional outbursts can be readily appeased with a few kind words and some understanding. Although this is a gentle, charming combination, these people lack self-confidence and are frequently taken advantage of by others.

Why Do Numbers Count

COMBINATIONS WITH A SOURCE NUMBER OF 3

No individual is simply one name or all of their names, although each name used will influence the overall personality and life experience as follows:

EXAMPLE 19.   3-7-1   Joella, Loretta, Madelaine, Natasha, Rosalyne, Roxanne, Alberto, Buck, Chuck, Gordon, Socrates, Woody, Yuri

These people have great opening lines but quickly run out of steam and haven't too much to say. They make great first impressions. They often enter business meetings with the firm resolve not to interrupt. But, if the meeting gets bogged down, the powerful 3 barges through the blunt 1, and, once again, they tread where angels fear to go. Fortunately, they are very resilient and can recover quickly from sticking their foot in their mouth.

Where the 1-2-3 is considered to be a desirable combination, the energy flow of the 3-7-1 restricts the vibrant, dynamic 3 from finding an outlet. As a result, the negative side of the 3 prevails and this combination can be very argumentative, forceful and self-centered. This combination is always starting over again from the beginning.

EXAMPLE 20.   3-8-2   Alana, Elinora, Katharina, Leona, Lisa-Maria, Lorraine, Aristotle, Buddy, Gus, London, Murphy, Osborn, Ulrick

This is a very bubbly quality that wants to be nice to everyone. They love people, parties, social events, and talking about anything. They love to party all night and hate to get up in the morning — any morning. Although, this is truly a delightful, gracious, fun loving quality to socialize with, from a result and production point of view, this combination is easy-going Joe (2-1-3) in reverse. Joe doesn't move forward very fast at all, so you can well image how productive he is in reverse!! In their desire to resolve conflict and maintain peace, they do not hesitate to stretch the truth. They like to tease as long as no one gets hurt. This combination is never at a loss for words.

EXAMPLE 21.   3-9-3   Carolyne, Charlotte, Katrina, Rozanne, Ruby, Sunny, Yoko, Alexander, Buzz, Judd, Justin, Monro, Quinn, Sloane, Uri

This combination is the unrestricted child running wild in the candy store. They are highly emotional and strive to appease their emotions with compulsive eating. They are wonderfully creative but seldom, if ever, complete anything. They can play music by ear and have an exceptionally strong voice that is superb for opera. This combination is the ultimate extrovert who has no idea of when or how to stop talking. They are completely unorganized and thrive on emotional drama. Life is strictly a game to be enjoyed — an excuse to have fun. They are possibly the world's worst housekeepers. These people are very subject to skin disorders such as rashes, acne, skin cancer, etc.

EXAMPLE 22.   3-1-4   Bunny, Constance, Georgina, Natalia, Rowena, Rusty, Ruth, Budd, Buz, Churchill, Duddy, Ludwig, Morrison, Wilbur, Yul

This combination takes the creative ability of the 3 and combines it with the precision and detailed skills of the 4. As a consequence, these people are outstanding at creating and sewing clothes and at all manner of hobbies. Their bubbly inner nature is thwarted by the placid 4, yet they always have a smile for everyone. They have a playful side but prefer the stability and tradition of home and family. They like to be productive and organized although sometimes the disorganized 3 can show itself behind cupboard doors.

EXAMPLE 23. 3-2-5 Adelaide, Caroline, Cornelia, Joanne, Roseann, Rubi, Susi, Cyrus, Fernando, Horace, Lorance, Quintin, Rudy, Russ

These numbers have many of the contradictions of the 2-3-5 combination but they have little desire to be nice. The 3 source loves a good argument and the 5 expression has no qualms about what it has to say. There is no loss for words here, nor is there any apology for what is said. In their opinion, they like to tease others. Unfortunately, their teasing is sarcastic and hurtful. Finishing projects is the last thing on these people's minds given that neither the 3 nor the 5 has any interest in completing what they start. There is a lot of energy and power in this combination and it is hard for them to sit still. They enjoy a wide variety of experiences with the opposite sex who are receptive to their vibrant personalities. Underlying their dashing charm is a great deal of vanity. These people are promoters who need plenty of freedom and variety to keep them busy but don't expect them to fill out any paperwork whatsoever.

EXAMPLE 24. 3-3-6 Dorothy, Jollean, Judy, Maryanna, Rosemary, Suki, Veronica, Cameron, Dunc, Dustin, Jaromey, Leonard, Norton, Ryun, Stu

The accountable and responsible instincts of the 6 draw out the positive aspects of the 3 and create a particularly congenial and wholesome personality. People with this combination have a superb sense of humour and, at the same time, they are very clear on their direction in life and on their goals. They prefer to do business in an easygoing manner but do not hesitate to back up their smile with conviction and strength. This is a completely balanced combination that offers the best of all possible worlds. They are artistic, creative, practical, and systematic. There is little they cannot do if they set their mind to it. They have a mature, robust, and well balanced physical appearance.

EXAMPLE 25. 3-4-7 Alanna, Amanda, Barbara, Lucy, Roberta, Rosalie, Trudy, Bronson, Burt, Colton, Connor, Dru, Kurt, Luis, Thornton

On first encounter, this combination begins with a 3 and appears to be a cheerful, gregarious, and vibrant personality expressing through the refined, poised, and dignified 7.

The second half of the story is less positive — capturing the argumentative, superficial, vain, and extravagant 3 source because the 7 expression internalizes rather than offers an outlet for the 3. Fundamentally, the energies are opposite — an extroverted source and an introverted expression. The push-pull of these opposite qualities offers a cheerful, optimistic, magnetic, and imaginative personality one moment and a superficial, vain, and whining nature in the next.

In the end, the 7 expression renders this combination very difficult to understand and hard to live with. Underneath their refined and congenial manner lives a surprisingly "tough cookie" who looks out for themselves. This can be particularly true of a Barbara if she is also called Barb which is a 1-4-5 combination. A barb is like a hook used for catching fish or hanging up meat — not a very pleasant image to identify with.

These are physically attractive people who have pleasant smiles and a difficult personalities to comprehend.

EXAMPLE 26. 3-5-8 Annemarie, Cassandra, Deborah, Georgia, Judi, Marjorie, Abraham, Aeron, Burc, Curt, Dusty, Geraldo, Guy, Kurtis

This is one of the four truly balanced combinations. The other three are 3-3-6, 6-9-6 and 6-2-8.

In this case, the magnetic, optimistic, gregarious, cosmopolitan, articulate, and imaginative 3 source finds expression through the 8 which is the number of material fruition. The 8 expression adds discrimination, balance, leadership, and efficiency to the 3 source. In other words, the 8 draws the 3 to completion and capitalizes on its imaginative, artistic, and entertaining qualities. The 8 insists on results and doesn't allow the 3 to become scattered, unfocused, or superficial.

EXAMPLE 27. 3-6-9 Carole, Joanie, Judith, Luci, Savanna, Tamara, Wenona, Angelo, Bud, Butch, Conroy, Curtis, Hunt, Orson, Pinkus

This is a musical, expressive, artistic combination that is always looking for an opportunity to serve and entertain others. Music, dance, drama, and the arts are an integral part of their lives. They are emotional, high strung, and can talk your ear off. For the most part, they are cheerful and bubbly, yet they often fall into the depths of complete despair. Lady luck, who is related to the lucky 3, bails them out at the eleventh hour just before everything is lost. Even so, their losses are substantial. This is a very scattered and disorganized quality that lives on inspiration. Although these people may not admit it, they love the drama of life. They have deep spiritual convictions and can verbalize their humanitarian instincts exceptionally well. They have a wonderful sense of humour and make good public speakers.

COMBINATIONS WITH A SOURCE NUMBER OF 4

No individual is simply one name or all of their names, although each name used will influence the overall personality and life experience as follows:

EXAMPLE 28.   4-6-1   Cleopatra, Georgianna, Lucia, Lucinda, Surina, Wonona, Cassius, Hercules, Juan, Klaus, Lukas, Rudyard, Vaughn

This is a physically strong and mechanical combination that loves to fix things and putter with their hands. Their narrow-minded nature reflects in their personality which is placid and not verbally expressive to say the least. This is a basic bread, meat, and potatoes person who has little or no sense of refinement. They have outstanding tenacity and endurance. They love to complete what they start as long as they can start over again from the beginning. In this sense, they are excellent house framers or roofers where they can repeat the same task day in and day out.

EXAMPLE 29.   4-7-2   Bruna, Dolora, Lucienne, Murial, Pomona, Susan, Utina, Ashburn, Claus, Garwood, Gustaf, Lucas, Reuben, Sullivan

These people have some good organizational skills but tend to be impractical when it comes to interfacing with life. They get hung-up on details and are often accused of being picky. They look to others to do the job for them and continuously run into differences of opinion and emotional upsets with the very people they most desire to please. They have a pleasant manner but lack inspiration and any sense of spontaneity. They strive very hard to be socially proper and, at the same time, they are somewhat defensive.

EXAMPLE 30.   4-8-3   Eleonor, Eunice, Juliette, Laurin, Leanora, Maud, Tatum, Aldus, Austin, Duncan, Harwood, Marcus, Tomasso, Uriah

In this example, the 3 energizes the 4 creating an inspired scientist who loves to talk about his technical insights and his latest invention. Mind you, this is the mad scientist with 10,000 incomplete inventions to his name. But he sure can tell a great story and bring a sense of vitality and aliveness to any mathematical equation. How so much technical know how and detail can live in such a messy environment is another of mother nature's mysteries. They tend to be loud both verbally and in their dress.

EXAMPLE 31.   4-9-4   Anastasia, Aubry, Donnamarie, Julina, Romona, Rosabella, Abdul, Donovan, Faust, Huntlee, Julian, Spaulding, Thurstan

Julian Bream, one of the world's master guitarists, embodies the technical perfection of this combination. He demonstrates all the 4's positive qualities — patient, practical, disciplined, intellectual, reliable, organized, and persevering. They can have outstanding powers of concentration. Others with the same combination could just as easily embody most of the 4's negative qualities — discontent, sceptical, narrow-minded, fussy, rigid, dogmatic, stubborn, dull, slow, and unproductive. Which side of the coin is reflected will be a function of childhood conditioning and current circumstances. Typically, they will embrace one side of this coin in certain activities and the opposite side in others.

EXAMPLE 32. 4-1-5 Anastassia, Georgiana, Hugette, Murielle, Prudence, Ursa, Arthur, Claud, Hagood, Horatio, Paolo, Paul, Salvatore

The analytical and intellectual qualities of the 4 are enlivened by the vibrant promotional nature of the 5. Where the 4 wants more data before making a decision, the 5 impatiently states that enough is enough and demands that a decision be made. This creates a much more progressive quality than most other combinations with a 4 source number. Unfortunately, they pay a price of internal struggle between indecision and impulsiveness. This can be an accident prone combination because the impulsive 5 wants change and travel whereas the 4 wants to stay at home and work on some organizational details. Consequently, when the 5 is speeding down the freeway and the 4 has its mind back at home, accidents happen. This combination does not accumulate many tangible results over a lifetime.

EXAMPLE 33. 4-2-6 Audry, Faun, Joenna, Lurleen, Roseanna, Ruthann, Uta, Artur, Audy, Barnum, Dagwood, Murray, Raymund, Truman

The 4-2-6 and the 6-7-4 are amongst the better combinations, given the wholesome, congenial, and responsible influence of the 6. Wherever the 6 is found, there is a strong tendency to bring out the positive qualities of the associated number.

This combination is intellectual, honest, trustworthy, loyal, organized, and persevering. They are excellent listeners and have outstanding analytical skills. Although they are a bit on the reserved side and don't like surprises or being spontaneous, they have a maturity that is inviting. They have a very strong love for home, family, and take an interest in community affairs.

They can be on the fussy side and worry a bit too much, but, all-in-all, this combination facilitates an attractive list of positives.

EXAMPLE 34. 4-3-7 Chiquita, Jacqui, Lauri, Lucilla, Maryruth, Susann, Ula, Antonio, Dustan, Gunar, Jonathon, Orlando, Quinlan, Ronaldo

This is a very analytical combination that is extremely hard to understand or get to know. The 7 expression shuts the door on the dull, fussy, dogmatic, and sceptical 4. They easily get stuck on small facts and refuse to discuss their feelings or anything personal. They have very limited verbal skills and a very placid, dull personality. In contrast, these people can be good technical writers or excel in theoretical mathematics and physics. This is an unhealthy combination subject to cancer and growths.

EXAMPLE 35. 4-4-8 Gertrude, Honoria, Julia, Luisa, Mauri, Mura, Suzette, Angus, Apollo, Durward, Enrique, Giuseppe, Gunthar, Saul

In this case the analytical 4 finds an effective outlet through the administrative, organized qualities of the 8 expression. The 8 and the 4 are in harmony with each other which draws out the more positive qualities of both numbers. This is a serious, hard working combination that is all business and not interested in social functions unless it will further business contacts. They are most content in the laboratory or the office, although they have an eye for good design and can enjoy a well constructed, quality home.

EXAMPLE 36. 4-5-9 Annamaria, Juliann, Oona, Rosamond, Shaun, Suzan, Una, Darius, Dugal, Guntar, Gustav, Hercule, Stuart, Theodore

4's and 9's don't go together well at all. Here, the 4 source is attuned to the subconscious (the underground) and is always in search of new and more data. The 4 quality hates to let go of anything regardless of it's obsolescence. In contrast, the 9 expression is all about letting go and surrender. Such action is blasphemy to the 4. This combination is exceptionally discordant and is prone to outbursts of anger and rage. In this example, the 9 intensifies the negative qualities of the 4. This is one of the least desirable of all the combinations.

The only combination which ends in a 9 and is not counterproductive is the 6-3-9. This combination functions effectively because the exceptional qualities of the 6 are sufficiently balanced not to be depleted by the 9 which insists on giving everything away.

COMBINATIONS WITH A SOURCE NUMBER OF 5

No individual is simply one name or all of their names, although each name used will influence the overall personality and life experience as follows:

EXAMPLE 37.   5-5-1   Becky, Christie, Edith, Meryl, Paulette, Peg, Rickie, Edwin, Desi, Gerry, Gilbert, Greg, Jed, Mitchell, Perry

The word "hell" is a 5-5-1 and aptly reflects just how difficult this combination is to endure. The enthusiastic, enterprising, freedom loving, and insightful 5 is thwarted by the 1 that is content with the basics of life. The 5 which is bursting at the seams to fly to the moon is weighted down and forced to keep both feet on the ground. Imagine a garden nozzle attached to a fire-fighting hose. The implication is a tremendous amount of pressure striving to get out of the tiny nozzle which causes the hose to be unmanageable and whip uncontrollably in all directions. This conflict is not necessarily apparent when observing people with this combination because the 1 expression always presents a solid, stable, consistent front. These people can be very creative, dynamic, and productive. These positives are sharply offset by the excessive stress that these numbers cause the physical body. This combination fosters very strong women, indeed.

EXAMPLE 38.   5-6-2   Bev, Bridget, Debby, Kelly, Mildred, Penny, Sydney, Winnie, Dennis, Eddy, Felix, Fredrick, Glen, Mike, Ted, Telly, Wes

The promotional, versatile, self-reliant, decisive, adventurous 5 is combined with the pleasant personality of the 2 creating a vibrant, dynamic nature that has some very good people skills. The 2 helps to take the sharp edge off the decisive, knife-edge of the 5. Yet, don't be fooled, behind the understanding, friendly presentation is a very determined, critical mind that can harbour some very strong, contemptuous, and bitter resentments. This is a moody combination that easily becomes depressed and filled with a sense of despair.

The name Mike is often well complimented by the name Michael which is a 6-9-6. In addition, Mike and Michael are often interchanged in conversation, whereas Ted is not often called Edward. Besides, Edward is a 6-4-1 which is not as desirable as the completely balanced 6-9-6 combination of Michael.

EXAMPLE 39. 5-7-3 Becki, Cicely, Del, Jillie, Laurette, Myrtle, Peri, Sherry, Ben, Gerri, Izzie, Ken, Mel, Melvin, Mickey, Reg, Shep

This is an exceptionally spontaneous nature that is never at a loss for words. The 3 loves to tease and make a game out of everything. Unfortunately, the knife-edge, critical nature of the 5 comes through and there can be a note of cruelty in their teasing. These people are outstanding promoters and always on the go. They are jacks of all trades and master of none. They seldom finish anything they start and have a hundred and one projects on the go at the same time. This is an impulsive and disorganized combination that will smile at you and do whatever they damned well please. Their creative and musical skills are outstanding.

Why Do Numbers Count

EXAMPLE 40.   5-8-4   Courtney, Debbi, Gwen, Jerry, Juanita, Monique, Trixie, Elvis, Jerry, Len, Lew, Merv, Neil, Percy, Sidney, Teddy

All the enthusiastic, decisive, enterprising, freedom loving qualities of the 5 are stagnated by the 4, creating a sceptical, narrow-minded, fussy, dogmatic nature that wants to get going but can't. This is a critical, moody, intolerant combination that pays the price with digestive and elimination problems. There is no real lack of intelligence here — they are simply stuck in a rut and they hate it.

EXAMPLE 41.   5-9-5   Jenny, Kimberly, Maureen, Nelly, Sheri, Vickie, Whitney, Cecil, Drew, Jimmie, Lewis, Ned, Terry, Trent, Wilfred

This is an intense combination that is well aware of their critical, moody, chaotic, temperamental, contemptuous, bitter, intolerant, and cruel nature. Consequently, they can be very strong disciplinarians and make a great effort not to lose emotional control because once they do, they have a terrible time reversing the outpour of negative spite. If they are at peace with their negative side, they can be exceptionally versatile, self-reliant, enthusiastic, insightful, and enterprising. This is a difficult combination to live because it offers a very fine line between total transformation and utter self-destruction.

These people are often hyper-active and find it impossible to sit still for five minutes. They cannot stand to be thwarted or repressed in any manner whatsoever. Even though they are exceptionally critical of others, they detest even the smallest amount of criticism directed to them. They are keenly aware of their own shortcomings and within their own minds they are constantly berating themselves.

Why Do Numbers Count

EXAMPLE 42. 5-1-6 Christine, Ginger, Kristine, Paula, Peggy, Jeri, Shirley, Benny, Clive, Erwin, Fred, Herb, Kenny, Timmie, Vincent

This is a vibrant, alive and dynamic combination. No moss grows under the feet of the 5 who has outstanding analytical skills and a determination to move forward at every opportunity. The 6 expression offers a clear channel for the aliveness of the 5. The 6 also helps to stabilize the 5 by adding an air of caution, responsibility, and accountability. Internally, these people are intense. Externally, they are congenial and progressive. They exude a great deal of confidence and trust in their lightning fast mental abilities. They have no fear of getting backed into a corner or of being taken advantage of in any way at any time. This combination is in the top 20% of all possible combinations.

EXAMPLE 43. 5-2-7 Cher, Fern, Jacqueline, Lynne, Meg, Nell, Susannah, Teri, Erich, Glenn, Henry, Kerby, Lenny, Mervyn, Seth, Willie

This is one of four particularly accident prone combinations. The others are 7-7-5, 4-1-5, and 5-8-4.

The 7 lives in a space beyond words and is focused on the more abstract and etherial qualities of life. Combined with the dynamic, challenging 5 that likes to do everything fast, including walking and driving, accidents occur because the 5 insists on fast movement and the 7 is often not focused on or connected to their physical reality.

The reasoning is slightly different, yet similar, for the 4-1-5 and the 5-8-4 combinations. In these cases, the 5 is always a-way-ahead of the 4 which has one foot stuck in the mud and is contemplating more data.

The 5-2-7 combination is exceptionally intelligent, high-strung, and sensitive. It is impossible to pin them down. They prefer to live alone and are very much their own person. They suffer from nervous, tense stomachs full of butterflies. When they visit a friend, they will rattle off a whole stream of insights and ideas. Before you have time to respond, they have wished you a good day and have vanished in front of your very eyes. They love the freedom of wide open spaces, the outdoors, nature, and travel. A fast car, a good stereo, and two weeks of non-stop driving is their idea of a good holiday.

EXAMPLE 44.   5-3-8   Beth, Betsy, Cheryl, Inger, Laura, Shelby, Susanna, Wendy, Bryce, Denny, Eric, Gregg, Keith, Louie, Tyler, Vince

This is a very quick, intelligent quality that effectively achieves results. They are a bit too intense for most people, but all in all this is a respectable combination. They can be prone to stuttering because the 8 expression supercharges the 5 source to the point that words can't keep pace with their thought process. This combination has a predisposition towards success and can be outstanding promoters and sales people. The 5 thrives on taking a stance for causes and the 8 is focused on justice which entices people with these names to work as lawyers or in the legal profession. These people can be gamblers because the impulsive 5 is combined with the 8 which wants the very best that money can buy.

Although this can be considered among the better combinations, the 8 expression number empowers the 5 source creating a fiery, no-nonsense personality. In comparison, the 5-1-6 combination which is similar to the 5-3-8 is more desirable because the 6 draws out the positives of the 5 in a congenial fashion creating a very wholesome, principled nature.

This combination is not recommended for a woman because it ends in an 8 which creates a strong external material focus and detracts from the inner female process.

EXAMPLE 45. 5-4-9 Bess, Betty, Blythe, Louise, Maura, Shelly, Tess, Vivien, Bert, Chet, Chevy, Ed, Fidel, Henri, Jeff, Les, Lyle, Red

In comparison to the 5-3-8, this combination is even more intense and, instead of culminating in success, they are plagued with personal and material losses. Like all combinations with a 5 source number, this combination hates to be repressed and can become particularly volatile when they don't get their own way. Underlying a somewhat flamboyant exterior, they have a naive trust in people. They deeply desire to assist people and are a champion of the underdog. Unfortunately, their high ideals are a constant source of disappointment for them. Their sarcastic bite stems from an underlying insecurity and a long history of perceived betrayals by life. They are aware of their naivety and it bothers them to no end when they forgo their first impressions and once again trust people they instinctively knew they shouldn't. In such a case, they will berate themselves a thousand times over before letting it go. This is also most distressing to them because both the 9 and the 5 want desperately to move on and be done with it.

COMBINATIONS WITH A SOURCE NUMBER OF 6

No individual is simply one name or all of their names, although each name used will influence the overall personality and life experience as follows:

EXAMPLE 46. 6-4-1 Cathie, Elsa, Eva, Faye, Kate, Lois, Mae, Stacey, Vera, Alfred, Bob, Bobby, Clifford, Edward, Frankie, Robb, Rod

This is a very capable, determined, responsible combination that does not mince a lot of words with their actions. They are honest and candid. They are very clear on what they want and are quite prepared to work for their goals. They like to be in charge of small groups such as a department in their office where they can participate in a leadership role. Although they have a deep love for home and family, they run their home more like a military academy than a home. Maternal instincts are present although the focus is on action and hard work. They are perfect candidates for the rank of a sergeant. This combination can suffer from headaches.

EXAMPLE 47. 6-5-2 Dianne, Doris, Jade, Jamie, Nadine, Paige, Robyn, Tracie, Andrew, Charlie, Cody, Gerald, Jared, John, Morris, Tony

These are very intelligent, capable, responsible people who are gracious and easygoing. They always have something pleasant to say about everybody and are a perfect choice for giving a toast to the bride or grace at the supper table. Their intelligence comes across in a smooth and friendly manner. They are excellent diplomats, combining a superb depth of mind with diplomacy and tact. As delightful as they are to be with from a social standpoint, living or working with them can be another matter because, in the end, they have a very definite tendency to procrastinate. Apart from their procrastinating ways, these people enjoy a wholesome, well-balanced personality.

EXAMPLE 48. 6-6-3 Alice, Allie, Bobbi, Claire, Debra, Frances, Isabel, Jackie, Jane, Jean, Jessica, Madge, Maxine, Meghan, Charles, Ethan, James, Jock, Lyndon, Sean, Tom

Like the 6-5-2 combination, these are very intelligent, capable, responsible people who have a gregarious, cosmopolitan, cheerful, optimistic, and magnetic personality. Unfortunately, they can have an argumentative, emotional nature that is hard to pin down and can be somewhat superficial. They love to quibble, tease, and generally argue the point. If you state what a beautiful clear day it is, they will likely take the opposite position to see if they can get a rise out of you. They are fun and playful but can truly be a trial to those looking for a commitment, definition, and decisions.

EXAMPLE 49. 6-7-4 Beverley, Hayley, Karen, Marcie, Melinda, Robin, Roslyn, Albert, Blake, Bradley, Dale, Fraser, Rory, Roy, Toni

On one hand, the innate intelligence of the 6 is supported by the intellectual skills of the 4 creating an exceptionally capable analyzer who does not tend to get lost in the detail — an analyzer who actually knows when to quit. On the other hand, the 4 is not expressive or spontaneous. This combination is on the reserved side, not favouring surprises or idle talk. The 4th physical sense is hearing. These people are superb listeners who portray a most sincere desire to understand other people's point of view. They have a non-threatening style of asking questions which combined with their ability to intelligently reflect on what they have heard, offers the other person a deep sense of being understood. They strive to understand and do not confuse their convictions with the opinions of others.

EXAMPLE 50.   6-8-5   Dolly, Eileen, Gayle, Janet, Jaye, Joy, Molly, Thelma, Bjorn, Clarke, Colt, Dave, Lloyd, Scott, Tommy, Wayne

This is a particularly vibrant and alive combination that thrives on newness, change, and travel. They are exceptionally quick of mind and could never be accused of having any grass grow under their feet. They are versatile, self-reliant, decisive, curious, enthusiastic, enterprising, freedom loving, adventurous, and very insightful. Not too many people are willing or capable of keeping up with this combination. Even so, there is a sense of sensibility infused in their character and a wholesomeness that is easy to admire. Life is not all roses for this combination given the 5 expression number which has intense likes and dislikes resulting in some bitter experiences and personal disappointments.

EXAMPLE 51.   6-9-6   Cecilia, Diane, Edna, Flo, Helga, Janice, Kaye, Mabel, Maggie, Marnie, Petra, Rae, Shelagh, Stella, Suzu, Tory, Alex, Dean, Don, Michael, Norm, Rolf, Troy, Victor, Wade

This is one of the few completely balanced combinations. It is the only combination where the source number and the expression number are equal and the combination can be considered balanced.

This combination is responsible, accountable, sensible, paternal, maternal, affectionate, artistic, stable, wise, congenial, and wholesome of character. They are most capable of doing anything they choose to do both artistic or practical. They create a wonderful home atmosphere and participate fully in community activities, offering their wisdom and support wherever they go. Sometimes they can be a bit on the bossy side and assume that they have all of the answers which is reflected in their favourite expression of "I know". They are so used to being tuned into a global knowingness, that even when they have no idea of what they are being told, they habitually interject "I know. Yes, I know." This habit is exasperating to those close to them.

All-in-all, this is a superb combination. They certainly make excellent counsellors and educators. Their only weakness stems from assuming too much responsibility for themselves and others. As a result, they can suffer from mental stress in the form of migraine headaches.

If Don is also called Donald, the 7-7-5 combination of Donald will create a more sensitive and intense quality to the degree it is used.

EXAMPLE 52.   6-1-7   Anne, Ashley, Gale, Glenda, Grace, Harriet, Hazel, Pearl, Darrell, Harvey, Marcel, Simon, Stewart, Walter, Warren

Although the 7 restricts the verbal expression of the 6 and adds a tone of reservation and caution, the 7 expression creates a refined, poised, and dignified personality with all the positive qualities of the 6 and few of the negative qualities of the 7. They are exceptionally intelligent and capable people although they keep a formal distance in personal relationships. They hold their body a bit on the stiff side and keep their head drawn back to signal that it is inappropriate for anyone to stand too close. They play their cards close to their chests and consider their personal affairs to be very private. It is difficult to really know someone with this combination. Their intelligence and dignity creates a strong cover personality that is initially hard to identify as a cover and is ultimately impenetrable.

EXAMPLE 53. 6-2-8 Bea, Brenda, Erika, Jasmine, Leah, Marge, Polly, Toby, Abe, Allen, Archie, Colin, Edgar, Floyd, Rob, Ross, Wallie

This is a superbly balanced combination in the sense that the 8 expression draws the energy of the 6 to a point of completion and fruition. Material success is typically substantial given that this combination begins with the capable, intelligent, responsible qualities of the 6 and completes with the discriminating and results oriented nature of the 8. These people have a very strong sense of commitment to home, family, business, and community. They stay clear, focused, and self-contained in times of conflict. This combination fosters an exceptionally capable administrator who embraces a deep sense of concern and respect for those who he manages. On a less positive note, the 8 doesn't add much humour or relaxation to the rather serious 6.

Although this is a balanced combination, it is very results oriented and is not suitable for everyone. This is especially true for women because the external material focus of the 8 is at odds with the energy of the internal female genitals. The administrative and material gains that this combination offers are typically offset by reproductive disorders for women using these numbers.

EXAMPLE 54. 6-3-9 Angie, Carmen, Erica, Holly, Jody, Lori, Patrice, Sheila, Charley, Earl, Gino, Keith, Harvie, Jake, Matthew, Ringo

The 9 draws out the artistic, musical, and community-minded qualities of the 6 and adds a flair of inspiration to an already wholesome and congenial nature. This combination has a strong humanitarian side that is generous, compassionate, and empathic. They have a good sense of rhythm and appreciate music. These people can have decisive moments of jealousy, temper, and possessiveness which pass rather quickly. Although they can worry extensively about the welfare of family, friends, and community, they always maintain an atmosphere of responsibility. This is one of the better first name combinations and possibly the ultimate surname combination as discussed in Chapter 22.

COMBINATIONS WITH A SOURCE NUMBER OF 7

No individual is simply one name or all of their names, although each name used will influence the overall personality and life experience as follows:

EXAMPLE 55. 7-3-1 Allison, Cora, Marjory, Maryanne, Melonie, Monica, Taylor, Arnold, Charlton, Gaylord, Jackson, Marlon, Pablo, Roland

Both the 7 and the 1 are very much their own person and not very communicative verbally. They demand a great deal of their own space and prefer to live on their own. On the other hand, the 7 loves to share moments of deep intimacy and can enjoy being very physical. When they are in such a mood, their haunting attractiveness is very alluring to the opposite sex. Given that the 1 also has a strong sex drive, this combination can find a great deal of satisfaction in sexuality. Unfortunately, exquisite moments of deep sexual union are followed by long periods of complete detachment which can leave the other party in utter confusion. Misunderstandings continuously result from the double message of "come here, go away". This is a recurring theme for most of the combinations beginning or ending in a 7. The theme is particularly strong in this example where the 7 is combined with the 1. These people are destined to lead a life of separation and detachment, only savouring the joys of relationship for brief periods. Loneliness is a familiar cry in their heart although they will not acknowledge it for long before they push forward in life ignoring their need for love and personal relationships.

EXAMPLE 56. 7-4-2 Dora, Leanna, Lynn, Margaret, Margot, Norah, Sonya, Ursula, Adolf, Caesar, Carlton, Mario, Noah, Omar, Oscar, Sly

This combination and its mirror image, the 2-4-7, are amongst two of the most sensitive, ungrounded, and confused of the 81 possible combinations.

The 7 lives in a world of abstraction where boundaries are loosely defined and words fail to capture the essence of their experience. The 2 expression is also short on boundaries and is sensitive and impressionable. The result is a very self-conscious personality that has little or no self-esteem. These people live in a world which is truly difficult for them or anyone to define. They are constantly concerned for their sanity during both awake and sleep times. Life for them is like a dream and it is a great struggle to tell what is real and what is not.

The 7-4-2 combination is more chatty than the 2-4-7 which can be almost invisible in nature. Both qualities are aloof, striving to protect their vulnerability, and at the same time desperate for affection which is a keynote of the 2 and a strong craving of the 7. Remember that 7's are very sensual and love intimacy but only for short durations because the vulnerability quickly becomes overwhelming. Where the 7-3-1 combination will bond strongly for short periods of time with long intervals between times of closeness, the 7-4-2 constantly lives in a push-pull struggle without relief. The physical wear of their vacillation drains their vitality and leaves them forever tired. These people are very late risers and can have little desire to talk before noon.

EXAMPLE 57. 7-5-3 Colleen, Deanna, Donna, Marianne, Nora, Pamela, Sharon, Amos, Dalton, George, Harrison, Jarod, Jerome, Norman

This numeric sequence is interesting to compare to the 3-4-7 combination in example 14. In the end, the 3-4-7 retracts upon itself and shuts the rest of the world out which leads to endless misunderstandings. In contrast, the 7-5-3 moves from introversion to extroversion. They draw from a source that is beyond words and are compelled to express what they are sensing and feeling. It's not an easy task but they give it a superb effort. *They wear their emotions on their sleeve* whereas the 3-4-7, who graciously smiles at the world, is very private and closed in the final analysis.

The 7-5-3's have their fair share of moodiness and introversion, yet they will come around in relatively short order and take another "kick at the cat" in an effort to find words for their feelings. When this quality is nervous, they will babble away to cover up their sensitivities. It's very difficult to determine how they will be from one moment to the next — one moment they will be the life of the party and the next they will go to their room and bury themselves in a book ignoring their own birthday party down-stairs. They have a very inquisitive nature and love to read. They can be perpetual students determined to find the answers to life, yet they are scattered in their efforts and seldom complete what they start. They bring a dramatic flair to everything they do.

Both the 7-5-3 and the 3-4-7 combinations are dealing with polar opposite forces which do not afford a life of harmony and nurturing relationships.

EXAMPLE 58.   7-6-4   Angela, Candace, Carol, Joan, Lola, Oprah, Shannon, Sonia, Carlo, Francois, Harold, Jacob, Lealand, Thomas, Walton

This is a difficult combination to live because the 4 does not offer the etherial, aloof 7 much of an outlet except in an analytical, detailed way. Since the 7 also has strong analytical skills, this combination can be very successful in research where abstract concepts are being formulated into tangible facts. They are also clever at electronics, accounting, and mathematics.

Where the 7 is finely tuned to the gentler elements of life, the 4 is very mechanical and intellectual. The result is a personality that is inspired but comes across in a stodgy fashion. They don't flow very well and find it hard to truly connect with people. Although their verbal skills are limited, intellectually they are very capable. Physically, they are prone to illness because they frequently suffer from indigestion and constipation.

EXAMPLE 59.   7-7-5   Amelia, Marlo, Morgan, Olivia, Rosalyn, Sonja, Sophia, Barron, Bradford, Brandon, Carlos, Donald, Jason, Marco

Not only is this one of the most accident prone of all the combinations, they have the weirdest accidents imaginable — a cupboard door pops open, a saucer falls out and hits the dish rack by the sink, flipping a knife off the counter into their little toe that then proceeds to become infected. Only if you have these numbers or live with someone with these numbers could you believe what happens to them.

This is an independent, very high strung combination, that runs on nervous energy and seldom sits still long enough for anyone to find out how they are. Besides, if you could physically pin them down, the ethereal 7 won't have words to capture their experience anyway. This combination devours books and all manner of information. They are wonderfully vibrant and alive but these numbers do not lend themselves to intimate, long-term relationships.

Under their vibrant exterior lives bitterness, resentment, jealousy, and depression. Their sharp, intense, and often arrogant nature is easily offended. They can be very self-righteous when hurt. This combination often meets with unexpected, sudden death through freak accidents or heart failure at an early age.

When Donald is called Don at the office and Donald at home, his experience will be relative to what he is called. This is true of many names which have common abbreviations.

EXAMPLE 60.   7-8-6   Lenore, Lisa-Marie, Lorna, Mary-Jane, Phoebe, Rhonda, Geoffrey, Harmon, Howard, Lyn, Malcolm, Mallory, Somerset

This is the only combination beginning with a 7 that has a wholesome balance to it. Why? The 7 is a very refined, delicate quality that needs a great deal of consistent support and understanding for it not to retreat inward and disconnect from the outer world. The 6 is the only number that has sufficient balance, stability, and insight to nurture the 7 into participating openly in life. The 6 draws out the philosophic, spiritual, mystical, inquisitive, refined, poised, and dignified qualities of the 7. At the same time, the 6 helps the 7 to remain practical in its inspiration rather than becoming deeply abstract and aloof. Even so, this is not an easy combination to live because the 7 is constantly striving to comprehend those qualities of life which go beyond words. They prefer a private, reserved life style. This combination is particularly astute at poetry, music, writing, and acting.

EXAMPLE 61.   7-9-7   Carolyn, Doreen, Marion, Mona, Naomi, Norma, Victoria, Anthony, Carroll, Crawford, Randolf, Roman, Sampson, Sloan

This is one of the three most difficult of all combinations to live within our world. The other two are 7-2-9 and 9-7-7.

Not only does the 7 expression draw from the crown chakra, the spiritual connection which is beyond words, but there is no outlet for the highly sensitized, inner experience through the 7 expression number. Everything, both positive and negative, that can be said about the 7 is amplified here. Unfortunately, the negative qualities tend to overshadow the positive qualities creating a very secretive, repressed, disconnected, pessimistic, aloof, nervous, and fearful personality that is deeply introverted. Their fragile, delicate nature is hurt *extremely* easily. For example, their sensitivity can amplify the slightest indiscretion of a loved one into devastating jealousy. *Walking on egg-shells* is an apt metaphor for the experience of living with a person using a 7-9-7 combination. They are secretive and private to an extreme. The sense of butterflies in their stomach is so strong that they are often shocked to be told that other people don't have the same experience. To them, butterflies and a nervous stomach are like a heart beating — it's simply part of living. This sensation can be so intense that they can spend a lifetime trying to cure what is diagnosed as an ulcerated stomach. Other names may take the edge off the 7-9-7 but under a somewhat poised and dignified exterior is a hyper-sensitive person who is under extreme stress.

Their lungs are particularly vulnerable to pneumonia and pleurisy. The slightest upset can take their breath away and cause a great deal of difficulty breathing. They can die without supposed warning because their calm exterior and private nature offer few, if any, clues to their inner turmoil.

They find their best relief in the out-of-doors and through writing, poetry, and music.

EXAMPLE 62.   7-1-8   Gloria, Jordan, Natalie, Noreen, Olga, Rosa, Sondra, Antony, Josiah, Mason, Riccardo, Rowan, Zacharie

This combination can be exceptionally shrewd in business. The 7 is superbly analytical and intuitive which, combined with the 8, moves the insights of the 7 to material success. Given that the 7 never gives anything away with facial expressions and both the 7 and 8 are very conservative with words, these people can be very active behind the scenes in the financial world and no one would ever know. If they choose to be in an administrative position, they will offer few words of advise, yet convey a strong message that no excuses will be tolerated for a lack of results.

They are clever, refined, dignified, confident, shrewd, and discriminating in everything they do. These people understand power and authority. They are completely self-contained and quite impossible to truly know.

EXAMPLE 63.   7-2-9   Fiona, Jeanna, Margo, Melodie, Monika, Nicola, Vanessa, Clayton, Geordie, Gerome, Hogan, Nicholas, Raymond, Waylon

A 9 expression number always intensifies the source number with which it is associated. In the case of the 7 which is already very sensitive, vulnerable, introspective, and aloof, the result is a hyper-sensitive, fearful, nervous, and very flighty personality. This combination is all ungrounded inspiration and dreams combined with humanitarian and religious ideals. They can be extremely jealous and suffer from deep, emotional mood-swings. Often they will strive to cover-up their extreme sensitivity by being talkative. Losses and misunderstandings are a constant plight of this combination. Although they appear to be much more extroverted than the 7-9-7 combination, they suffer from all of the same stress and frustrations.

COMBINATIONS WITH A SOURCE NUMBER OF 8

No individual is simply one name or all of their names, although each name used will influence the overall personality and life experience as follows:

EXAMPLE 64. 8-2-1 Carolina, Joanna, Lurline, Rosanna, Roxana, Rubie, Susie, Burgess, Burnett, Johnathan, Montgomery, Murrey, Quentin

This is a hard-nosed business personality from the old-school — get a bigger hammer if it doesn't work the first time. There is no lack of determination, will, and obstinance here. This self-centered personality is interested in results and has no concern for the feelings and personal needs of others. Although the tendency is to be unscrupulous, calculating, and materialistic, they can be true pioneers for justice and truth with no fear of being blunt and demanding. These people crave material success but seldom, if ever, get off the ground — they are forever pioneering new ventures and beginning once again from square one. This combination needs the support of offsetting numbers in other names to soften their hard-hitting, material focus. Like the 1-7-8, this combination is very hard on a woman's internal female process and can cause reproductive disorders.

EXAMPLE 65. 8-3-2 Bunnie, Lucille, Pollyanna, Rolanda, Ronalda, Tomasina, Boothe, Currie, Elwood, Hubert, Jonathan, Rooney, Rustie

In contrast to the previous example, this very smooth business personality has excellent people skills and can readily solicit the help of others. Unfortunately, the desired results are seldom achieved because these people tend to be too trusting in others and too empathic toward their employees. They allow personal issues to be confused with business needs. These people attract excellent business opportunities but seldom are willing to work hard enough to fulfill their contractual obligations. There is always someone to blame for the loss of their material dreams. They adore all the material conveniences of modern day living and fantasise about yachts and mansions with servants and gourmet chefs.

EXAMPLE 66. 8-4-3 Brooke, Julie, Luise, Margareta, Rosalee, Trudey, Quenby, Armando, Derwood, Gunther, Jurgen, Romeo, Roscoe, Ulysses

This strong personality can be most convincing with their verbal skills. There is a tendency to be indulgent in food, drink, and sexuality. Their appetite for both quantity and quality will show early in life around their waistline. Even so this is a cheerful, magnetic, vital combination that would do very well if they could learn not to scatter their efforts. They constantly promote their business by entertaining their clients and suppliers. They love to give extravagant parties where no expense is spared. This is a go-for-broke personality with a belief in living for today, for tomorrow you may die. They like to gamble with life. The 3 expression scatters the administrative and executive focus of the 8, limiting their accomplishments.

EXAMPLE 67. 8-5-4 Annamarie, Isadora, Jude, Judie, Oriana, Rosemarie, Bruce, Buster, Hughe, Jules, Luke, Miguel, Theodor

This combination combines an administrative sense with a particularly good eye for facts and figures which stands them well in the business and scientific worlds. They are exceptionally patient with a strong bent for results. Although they are slow to move and decide, they are exceptionally thorough and absolute sticklers for detail. Their nature is steady, reserved, practical, and persevering. Behind their discerning, placid nature is a very self-confident identity. Their dogmatic and stubborn streak can only be appeased with solid business logic. They are tight-fisted with money and likely have been accused of being a penny pincher more than once or twice in their life. They are particularly good at mathematics and physics.

Their love of rich foods runs into difficulty with the 4 which holds onto everything creating gastro-intestinal problems. They are also very subject to gout given their liking for rich foods, poor digestion, and slow elimination.

EXAMPLE 68.   8-6-5   Coralee, Joana, Juliet, June, Loralee, Lucie, Trudie, Duke, Ellwood, Huey, Hunter, Huxley, Tulley, Quent

This is a very strong, self-reliant, versatile combination that doesn't take no for an answer from anyone. This quality wants results and they want them now. They are not much fun to live with when they don't get what they want. When their callous and bitter side comes out, they have little trouble telling people what they think or feel or where to go in no uncertain terms. They are inclined to be impatient and know-it-alls. They are often accused of having very thick skin. In their own minds, they do not see themselves as defiant and head-strong as people perceive them to be.

They have an abundance of energy and have a hard time sitting still. They love change and travel especially when they can go first class. Their impulsive nature undermines their innate business sense.

Women with this combination have difficulty with personal relationships because they are forever trying to control the relationship and be the boss. A woman with these numbers would always wear the pants in her home.

EXAMPLE 69. 8-7-6 Antoinette, Morgana, Muriel, Pandora, Roxanna, Susen, Boone, Dustie, Humphrey, Huntley, Purcell, Ruben, Tucker

Once again, here is a combination that ends in a 6 and should be considered in the top 20% of the 81 possible combinations. In comparison, the 6-2-8 fits into the top 5% because the source number of 6 starts with substantial, wholesome, mature ideas and cultivates the intention to a point of fruition. The weakness of beginning with an 8 source number is that expansive, far-reaching goals are continuously upgraded before they are initiated. The challenge of the less ambitious 6 expression number is to keep up with the ever expanding goals of the 8. This pattern tends to overwhelm the 6 and frustrate the 8 who wants results relatively immediately. Even so, it should be kept in mind that the 6 demands responsibility and is determined to maintain an air of sensibility in all things. Sometimes it is overlooked that the 8 has a strong sense of balance in its own right. Hence, this combination works out much better than most and exudes an air of balance in both home and business.

EXAMPLE 70. 8-8-7 Carlota, Darla-Jo, Dolores, Eleanor, Elenora, Lavonna, Buckley, Edmund, Guthrie, Leopold, Redmund, Russell

In this example, all the positive qualities of the 8 are kept in close check by the 7 expression number which plays its cards close to the chest. As a result, this can be a very shrewd business combination that attracts excellent opportunities but never experiences complete success in anything they do. They can come within a hair's breath of success but somehow they can never quite close that final, small gap. Why? It's the nature of the 7 to discover the secrets of life but it takes the 8 to make the theory practical and material. Because the energy flow goes from the 8 to the 7, goals are never fully realized. When a combination ends in an 8, goals and objectives flourish and grow to material and spiritual success.

EXAMPLE 71. 8-9-8 Alexandra, Georgetta, Justine, Ramona, Rosalina, Suzie, Dudley, Julien, Monroe, Rupert, Sherwood, Woodie, Zeus

On the surface, this may appear to be the ultimate business combination, yet this is another example where too much of a good thing is not healthy. Remember, the upside of the 8 is justice whereas the downside is injustice.

This combination attracts huge business opportunities where the game rules are centered around shrewd materiality and power. They love the world of high finance, banking, economics, and politics. These people play for keeps and will not hesitate to unscrupulously exercise obscure options found in the fine print of contracts. Manipulation and exploitation are common bed partners of these numbers. Take heed and do not be tempted to use this combination for a business name.

These people love quality and quantity to the extreme and suffers from a constant diet of rich, gourmet foods. They are prime candidates for gout, which is excruciatingly painful.

EXAMPLE 72. 8-1-9 Augusta, Carlotta, Johanna, Magnolia, Ruthie, Sue, Yolanda, Buddie, Cooper, Culver, Currey, Shakespeare, Woodley, Yule

This is an attractive combination in the sense that the 8 has a strong sense of justice, confidence, authority, and leadership. They have a clear perception of life and how it works. When combined with the humanitarian, and inspirational nature of the 9, the result is a strong and inviting personality that can express themselves with outstanding insight in both business and the arts. Unfortunately, where the 8 attracts superb business opportunities, the humanitarian ideals of the 9 lose or give away all of the profits earned. Combinations which *end* in a 9 also *end* in losses both personally and materially. In this case, the losses are substantial because both the 8 and the 9 have very high ideals and are striving to achieve significant goals in life.

| COMBINATIONS WITH A SOURCE NUMBER OF 9 |

No individual is simply one name or all of their names, although each name used will influence the overall personality and life experience as follows:

EXAMPLE 73.   9-1-1   Cindy, Christin, Iris, Kirstin, Kristin, Nicki, Suzanne, Claude, Gil, Irwin, Nick, Phillip, Skip, Timmi, Wilt

These people have high ideals and wonderful intentions but lack outlets for their dreams. The humanitarian, universal ideals of the 9 are tapered down to the single, independent, detached reality of the 1. The result is tension in the head, throat, and nervous system which gives way to confusion, dizziness, frustration, and fits of temper. The metaphor of a huge fire hose with a garden nozzle outlined in Example 37, is also applicable to this combination. The extreme polarity difference between the 9 and the 1 will eventually take its toll on health and personal success.

EXAMPLE 74.   9-2-2   Audrey, Ivy, Liz, Mindy, Phyllis, Raquel, Sue-Ann, Trish, Beau, Doug, Guido, Kirby, Maurey, Rich, Saunders, Will

In comparison to the 2-9-2 in Example 10, this combination is more lively and willing to participate in life. Yet, the universal ideals of the 9 find little tenacity in the 2 expression, resulting in a very easy going, laid back, likable personality. It is very difficult for them to say no to anyone asking for help. They are emotional, gentle dreamers who lack will power to follow through with their intentions. They are lost outside of relationship and always seek the approval of others. The 2 quality always has a tendency to turn food into fluids which results in overweight, even on a conservative diet.

EXAMPLE 75.   9-3-3   Christy, Cindi, Eugenie, Jacquie, Kris, Kristy, Laurie, Chris, Eugene, Laurier, Leonardo, Lou, Ricky, Willis

This is a very inspired personality that can talk a mile a minute. They are extreme extroverts, full of fun, laughter, optimism, and imagination. They can play music by ear and have a strong, melodious lilt to their voice. They have a magnetic personality that loves to tease and is hard to resist. Their weakness lies in being too fun-loving. They tend to scatter their efforts and have an extremely hard time organizing themselves let alone others. They are never on time and will somehow manage to be late for their own funeral. Underlying their bubbly nature is a very spiritual focus with exceptionally high humanitarian ideals. They can suffer from extreme mood swings. The best way to get them out of the depths of depression and despair is with love, affection, and any old corny joke.

EXAMPLE 76.   9-4-4   Beulah, Bibi, Kitty, Lily, Missy, Sybil, Vi, Winny, Audie, Clint, Cyril, Jacques, Julio, Kirk, Louis, Rudolf

This combination becomes ecstatic when they see a spiritual idea manifest in physical reality. They will often skip and dance about when such events occur which is quite in contrast to their otherwise stodgy personality. Unfortunately, this is a difficult combination to live because the idealistic, unconditional 9 is forced to express through the placid, intellectual 4 that is never quite ready to make a decision. This robs the 9 of its spontaneity and destroys many inspired dreams. The frustration of the 9 compounds the overall problem and the 4 degenerates into being fussy, stubborn, and unproductive. Once the catch-22 cycle starts it becomes exceptionally difficult to break. These people can be extreme perfectionists regarding the smallest of details. This is one of the least desirable combinations and is not offering any favours for those who choose to use it.

EXAMPLE 77.   9-5-5   Beula, Gigi, Glynis, Julianne, Kristi, Liby, Mitzi, Ricki, Bing, Jim, Flin, Philipp, Rick, Sid, Virgil, Wilf, Woodrow

The inspired 9 and the versatile and impulsive 5 create a medium to large tornado of activity around these people. There is a great deal of impatience and intensity here which can be exhausting for those living with them. Seldom are they overweight because they run on nervous energy even when they are sitting still. Don't cross these people because they will seek revenge. They can be very strong disciplinarians in an effort to avoid their contemptuous and cruel streak that can express when they lose control. They attract many bitter experiences in life which is difficult for them to understand given the humanitarian ideals of their hearts. This is a high strung, self-reliant, promotional nature which starts a thousand and one projects and never finishes any. There is no lack of mental agility here.

The name Jim is offset by the name James, 6-6-3, to the degree Jim is also called James.

EXAMPLE 78.   9-6-6   Claudine, Ginny, Kim, Laurel, Lil, Pauline, Tilly, Trixy, Billy, Britt, Dirk, Griffin, Hugo, Skippy, Tim, Vik

This is one of the more delightful and wholesome combinations available. It is referred to in Chapter 23 in the discussion of destiny combinations. This combination offers the best of many worlds because the accountable, responsible, and sensible 6 draws out all of the positive qualities of the 9. In this case, the humanitarian and altruistic nature of the 9 finds expression in unconditional love, forgiveness, compassion, empathy, and tolerance. Plus all the intuitive, musical, artistic, and visionary qualities of the 9 are enhanced by the 6 expression. The result is a well balanced, affectionate, artistic, stable, wise and congenial nature that embraces life and achieves their goals.

EXAMPLE 79.   9-7-7   Guinevere, Ingrid, Jill, Lilly, Liv, Mimsy, Nikky, Vicky, Bruno, Irving, Jimmy, Kin, Maurice, Philip, Smitty, Vic

Once again, this is one of the most difficult of all combinations to live. Two other very similar combinations are the 7-2-9 and the 7-9-7. In this example, the 7 restricts the expression of the 9 offering little or no outlet for the inspiration and enthusiasm of the source number. The 9 which is high-strung and somewhat nervous to begin with is not well complimented by the 7 which is sensitive, delicate, and vulnerable to all the subtle energies of life. These people have much to offer but it is difficult for them to feel safe enough to share what they feel. They have a tendency to be somewhat tight-lipped. They enjoy expressing themselves in art, music, and writing. When they get a common cold, it settles immediately in their lungs and care must be taken that it doesn't turn into pneumonia. In addition, this combination can suffer from nervous disorders, given the high level of sensitivity of both the 9 and the 7. These people crave affection and understanding, yet are forced to live a very lonely life. They can be intelligent and well read with exceptional writing skills.

EXAMPLE 81. 9-8-8 Kristyn, Lauren, Lizzy, Maude, Milly, Mimi, Trixi, Vikki, Bill, Dwight, Lauren, Mitch, Samuel, Skipp, Slim, Timmy

The universal ideals of the 9 strive to find expression through the 8 in the material world. Ask these people how they are doing and they will tell you about the big business deal that didn't quite make it. But there is one cooking now that will be "the big one", putting them on easy street for the rest of their lives. The 9 quality is inspired and visionary but lacks the practicality to put their ideals into action. The 8 expression helps this process considerably. Unfortunately, the 8 desires outstanding material success and between the two of them, they get carried away with schemes to become billionaires. They want immediate results and lack the patience and willingness to make the effort required to achieve their goals. Remember, the 8 is an administrator and not the worker. These people can have an air of being pompous and good-natured at the same time.

Although this is not a recommended combination for a first name, it does work effectively for a destiny combination that is the result of other balanced names as discussed in Chapter 23. To work towards and include significant humanitarian and material goals in one's life is unquestionably desirable as long as such goals are not all consuming to the exclusion of personal and family needs.

EXAMPLE 81. 9-9-9 Jacquelyn, Laurell, Luella, Lilli, Micki, Nikki, Vicki, Chip, Cliff, Dick, Dougy, Duane, Gib, Mick, Phil, Willy

In this example, all the qualities of the 9 are embraced in full force. As humanitarian, loving, and altruistic as these people are, they can be equally as possessive, jealous, selfish, and unforgiving. They can change from moment to moment, swinging from the heights of inspiration to the depths of self-pity and vile temper. This combination is dramatically influenced by the other names with which it associates. These people usually specialize in professional careers and can be extreme perfectionists. They tend to seek careers where they can fulfil their humanitarian ideals and serve people.

The lesson of the 9 is to let-go, surrender, and forgive. If they make any effort to hold onto loved ones or material things, they are taken from them or they lose them. They must walk a fine line of detachment which is extremely exasperating because they love so dearly and deeply. This apparent contradiction results in a sense that life is unfair. They can find it particularly difficult to understand how their love for their family is seen as smothering and possessive.

The 9 represents the full and complete self on the material plane. If they find balance, they can be true humanitarians and live a full and rewarding life.

PART V

ANALYZING NAMES & BIRTHDATES

CHAPTER 18 — HOW TO ANALYZE ALL YOUR NAMES

The most important names in your life are the names that you are called.

The more frequently you are called certain names, the more impact they have on your life.

Although the names that you are called have the greatest impact, all of the names on a birth certificate have an influence. Even your mother's maiden name is a vital component of your character. Why? We are primarily raised by mothers who acquired their formative attitudes, beliefs, and discipline from *their* mothers. Given that we all acquire ninety percent of our attitudes in the first seven years of life, a mother's upbringing is a framework for her contextual perception of life through which she trains her children.

So, where do we draw a practical line to identify the significant influences and keep the parameters within manageable proportions. First, let's define three primary components of names in the following example:

$$\begin{array}{ccccccc}
 & 6 & & & 2 & & 8 & (6+2=8) \\
\text{John} & 5 & + & \text{Doe} & 4 & = & 9 & (\underline{5}+\underline{4}=\underline{9}) \\
 & 2 & & & 6 & & 8 & (2+6=8)
\end{array}$$

Personal + Family = Destiny

John's **personal** nature is a 6-5-2.

John's **family** nature is a 2-4-6.

John's **destiny** nature is an 8-9-8.

DESTINY COMBINATION

The destiny combination is the sum of the personal and family combinations.

When two forces combine, a resolve between the two is created which becomes the unified direction of influence. Can you recall your high school geometry when force A was added to force B and the resulting vector was force C which determined the direction of the moving object? Given two names, the resulting direction and force of the two vectors is called the destiny combination. The destiny combination is the matrix sum of the personal and family combinations.

Sometimes, very strange twists of fate arise with the destiny combination. People can have very strong, capable, dynamic personal and family combinations which add up to a very passive, lazy destiny combination that never culminates in material success. In this case, great talent can vaporize into thin air. Consider the following example of personal, family, and destiny combinations:

$$\begin{matrix} 6 \\ 9 \\ 6 \end{matrix} + \begin{matrix} 5 \\ 1 \\ 6 \end{matrix} = \begin{matrix} 2 \\ 1 \\ 3 \end{matrix}$$

Both the 6-9-6 and the 5-1-6 are particularly competent, responsible and accountable people. Yet, their abilities vaporize in passivity and indulging in good times and too many parties.

Sometimes, very passive, unambitious personal natures combined with stressful and chaotic family combinations result in the Midas Touch and everything turns into gold. Consider the following example of personal, family, and destiny combinations:

$$\frac{\frac{2}{1}}{3} + \frac{\frac{2}{3}}{5} = \frac{\frac{4}{4}}{8}$$

A 4-4-8 destiny is not the combination of a corporate giant, but it is a tenacious, determined, practical quality with a predisposition to success. In this example, the level of success achieved will appear to exceed the personal and family qualities.

FAMILY NAME(S)

All the people within a given family have similar personality traits. Some people fit the family mould better than others. For example, some people are the white sheep of the family and some are the black sheep. Some are a chip off the old block and others rebel at the family norm. Even so, family traits are present in all families and **personal** combinations depict how the individual fits the **family** personality.

When analyzing an individual, an effective place to begin is with their family nature. People can often recognize their family, particularly the negative aspects, more readily than they can recognize their personal nature within the family. In the case of a married woman, it works well at this point to compare and contrast the differences between the nature of her family of origin and her current experience. This comparison will often shed light on how her personality changed after she married into a different family personality.

PERSONAL NAME(S)

Because an individual's personal nature can be dramatically different from their background, it can be very insightful to compare and contrast the two names. Where traits are similar, they will be enforced and amplified. Where there are contradictions, the individual will respond differently from one experience to the next. Don't strive to describe a consistent, homogeneous personality. Paradox and contradiction are normal in this physical experience called life.

OTHER NAMES

Nicknames are common and, combined with a family name, they create their own destiny combination. As children, we often have nicknames which are not used outside of the family. Certainly, we all feel different with family members in comparison to being with casual friends. Analyzing the family nickname in comparison to the accepted given name can point out differences between the context of the family system and the public image.

One's business signature on cheques and legal documents is often different from one's common names or one's legal names. Computing the business signature will identify one's experience with legal documents and business affairs. The business signature is a secondary influence and less important than what one is commonly called.

The full legal name is like a blueprint underlying one's everyday experience although it is very much a secondary influence to one's common names and for all practical purposes should be ignored.

CHAPTER 19 — BIRTHDATES & THE INNER SELF

Some say that the planets and the stars exert a force upon the affairs of humankind. Although this is true, the more important consideration is their position which reflects the symbolic qualities of changing energies in our universe. The planets and the stars are like large iron filings on a table top held in position by enormous forces beyond our comprehension. The patterns formed in any given moment tell us about the energies at play in that moment. In conjunction with this perspective, each of us choose a moment of birth in order to embrace a certain quality of energy to assist us in having a specific pattern of experiences.

The essence of one's choice is earmarked by one's birthdate. When you were born, there existed a unique flavour or tone to life — whatever the spiritual essence was the day you took your first breath of life, signals the spiritual essence of your **Inner, Spiritual Self**. The innate, spiritual essence within strives to grow and express through the vehicle of the physical body and the mind. If the mind and/or the body are confused and not functioning properly, the Inner Self will be unable to express clearly and freely. Hence, one's spiritual growth will be thwarted and fulfilling one's life purpose will be frustrated.

A metaphor for mind, body and spirit is a movie projector forming an image on a screen, called the screen of life. The Inner Self is denoted by one's month, day, and year of birth. The Inner Self is

always considered to be pure and divine, and *no date of birth is better or less desirable than another.* The qualities of the mind are influenced by one's names. The names are like the focus on the projector. If the projector is out of focus, the purity of the Inner Self will not form a clear picture on the screen of life.

Consequently, it is vital that the name be in harmony with the birthdate and allow free expression of the Inner Self. If the names are not in harmony with the birthdate, confusion and internal conflict will give way to dysfunction, sickness, and serious complications. When analyzing names, take note of this consideration of the balance between the Inner Self and the names used. **When the names and the Inner Self are in conflict, the person will focus on the negative qualities of the names rather than the positive qualities.** In such cases, the person can be totally out of touch with their Inner Self and will not recognize the qualities of their inner potential. Anyone who is out of touch with their Inner Self will be discordant and have no sense of their personal needs. As a consequence, they will tend to compromise and betray themselves and others and will be totally confused as to why life is difficult and full of misunderstandings for them. Often they will express sentiments like, "What have I done that was so bad that I deserve this?"

Even though names and birthdates are not the whole story of life, they are a significant component. Possibly, they constitute the border of the puzzle of life and offer a framework for the individual experience. Within the framework there exists many more pieces to the puzzle. It's critical to understand family of origin psychology as discussed in Chapter 21 otherwise changing names can be no more than putting a bandaid on old wounds that need attention before they are dressed.

Balanced name combinations are presented in Chapter 22 for those interested in changing their names, their children's names, or the name of their business.

LIFEPATH

The path we choose to take on the journey of life is dramatically influenced by our birthdate. This path, called a **lifepath**, is a composite of the month, day, and year of birth. Notice that the month is stated first. Consider the following example:

April 24, 1952

4   6   8

The month of **4** = **4**

The day of   **24** = 2 + 4 = **6**

The year **1952** = 1 + 9 + 5 + 2 = 17 = 1 + 7 = **8**

The rules for reducing the numbers to a single digit are the same for the sum of the vowels and consonants as noted in Chapter 14.

The lifepath in this example is 4, 6, 8. This person's journey will take them down 4th Avenue, across 6th Street, and then down 8th Avenue. In this example, 4, 6, 8 are focus areas for this person during their life journey.

MAJOR & MINOR LIFE FOCUSES

When the 3 focus numbers are added together, they identify a 4th number called the **Major Life Focus.** In comparison, the month, day, and year of birth are called **Minor Life Focuses.**

In our example, the Major Life Focus for April 24, 1952 is:

4 + 6 + 8 = 18 = 1 + 8 = **9**

The **Major Life Focus** is the overriding focus of the Lifepath — it is a fixed constant throughout a person's life. Using the above example, one's life journey through a city would consist of going down 4th Avenue, across 6th Street, and then down 8th Avenue, all of which will be viewed or perceived from the overall context of the 9 Major Life Focus.

Consider the metaphor of a sunset over a lake surrounded by rolling hills. The scene is made up of many colors including a brown sandy beach, blue water, and dark green trees on the rolling hills, plus a pink hue from the setting sun which permeates all of the colors. The overall pink hue is like the major life focus — it is constant in the whole picture. The green, brown, and blue are **always present**, yet they will be more or less predominant if your focus is on the water versus the beach or the trees.

In this sense, the **Minor Life Focuses** have an interesting influence on one's life. Each minor life focus primarily affects one's life for a period of 27 years:

The **month** primarily affects life from birth to 27 years of age.
The **day** primarily affects life from 27 years of age to 54.
The **year** primarily affects life from 54 years of age until death.

The word **primarily** has been used extensively in defining the effect of the minor life focuses. In fact, all the minor life focuses effect one's life experience all the time. **The most impactful minor life focus is the second minor defined by the day of birth.**

The first, second, and third minor life focuses are abbreviated in the following manner for ease of discussion:

First minor = month of birth = first minor life focus
Second minor = day of birth = second minor life focus
Third minor = year of birth = third minor life focus

Using our example of April 24, 1952 and taking into account the major life focus and the changing minors, the following definitions apply:

From birth to 27, this person is a **9 living under the influence of a 4.**
From 27 to 54, this person is a **9 living under the influence of a 6.**
From 54 until death, this person is a **9 living under the influence of 8.**

Stated in more condensed terms:

From birth to 27, this person is a	**9 under a 4.**
From 27 to 54, this person is a	**9 under a 6.**
From 54 to death, this person is a	**9 under an 8.**

Are you confused yet? It's not as difficult as it looks. In this example, the major life focus is a 9 and is constant for their entire life. As they grow older and the minor life focus changes, so will their personality and life experiences. As a 9 major life focus, their Inner Self will always be inspirational, intuitive, musical, artistic, generous, and compassionate.

From birth to 27 years of age, the first minor of 4 will add the qualities of being analytical, practical, reliable, disciplined, organized, and persevering. The two qualities combined create an inspired personality who is very practical.

From 27 to 54, the qualities of the second minor of 6 will be amplified and the person will become more congenial, affectionate, and artistic. During this period, the second minor of 4 will be de-emphasized.

From 54 on, the third minor of 8 will bring into play the qualities of administrator, leadership, and material appreciation, and the second minor will become de-emphasized.

Let's consider another example:

July 8, 1946.

7 + 8 + 2 = 8

The minor life focuses are 7, 8, 2. The major life focus is an 8.

From birth to 27, this person is an **8 under a 7.** The 8 tells us this person will be confident, discriminating, shrewd, ambitious, efficient, and results-oriented. The 7 will influence the 8 by being introspective, reflective, calm, refined, poised, dignified, insightful, sensitive, and generally very private.

From 27 to 54, this person will be an **8 under and 8.** The minor life focus that affects one's life between 27 and 54 is the most significant, minor life focus. In this example, the major life focus is an 8 and the minor focus from 27 to 54 is an 8. Consequently, the second minor of an 8 will particularly amplify all of the 8 qualities of confidence, ambition, leadership, thoroughness, efficiency, and material appreciation. The reserve and the privacy of the 7 will become a minor influence.

From 54 until death, this person will be an **8 under a 2.** This will be a dramatic shift from being private and reserved for their first 27 years and then very results-oriented and business minded for the next 27 years, to becoming very much a people person when they turn 54. For the first 54 years, intimate, personal relationships were secondary to the qualities of an 8 under a 7 and of an 8 under an 8. Yet, a minor life focus of a 2, will shift the individual's focus to being sensitive, cooperative, considerate, adaptable, responsive, nurturing, and very interested in spending great quantities of time with people. The 8 would spend time with people to acquire desired results. The 2 thrives on spending time with people simply for the pure pleasure of sharing the nuances of human nature. Such a change in attitude may take this person and their friends by surprise, to say the least.

Typically, we mellow with age and become more relaxed and open. This generality is not true for someone going from a first minor of a 2 to a second minor of a 5, or, for someone going from a first minor of a 3 to a second minor of a 7. It's always easier and more fun to analyze people who have made such radical shifts in their life — particularly when they have not followed the logical progression of maturing with age.

The total number of combinations of the lifepath is a multiple of the 9 possible numbers in each of the 3 minor life focuses:

9 x 9 x 9 = 729 combinations.

The total number of name combinations is a multiple of the 9 possible vowel totals and the 9 possible consonant totals:

9 x 9 = 81 combinations.

When these 729 combinations are combined with 81 possible first name combinations, 81 possible surname combinations, 81 possible destiny combinations, plus the variations of nicknames and maiden names, the puzzle begins to become complex. All of these considerations are also woven into cultural, family, and educational belief systems. No wonder every person on planet earth is unique.

The next chapter deals with how to resolve the various influences of the birthdate and all the names — how to put it all together.

CHAPTER 20 — RESOLVING ALL THE NUMBERS

No single person is simply their name. No one is simply a John or a John Doe born at a certain time. Yet, the names that one uses and one's birthdate are part of the complex tapestry of life that includes hereditary, family-of-origin conditions, prevailing social, political and economic environment, education, diet, exercise, personal experiences, etc.

Within this complex tapestry, the name John colors the picture as do all of John's names, birthdate, and personal yearly cycle. Each name adds or subtracts from the sum total of John's experience and contributes to the net result of who John is.

To resolve all the components, pursue personal analysis in three stages.

First, analyze each component of the equation separately and independent of the other components.

Second, compare and contrast the various components. When one name is all graciousness and another is radically independent and intolerant, don't hedge on describing the two qualities. Point out the contradiction of how the person in question responds differently to the same circumstance. Reflect on the internal struggle of deciding which way to react — or at the annoyance of responding one way one time and in a completely different way another time.

Third, strive to summarize and bring the loose ends together. In this step, trust your intuition given that you are well tuned to the individual by this point. Don't be overly concerned about finding one simple net personality for the person you are analyzing.

People are not simply one way. The basic design of life on planet earth is one of polarity, contradiction, and paradox. Almost everyone lives with many contradictions and paradoxes in their lives.

Each personal analysis should address the following components in the order they are listed:

1. Personal cycle.

2. Surnames vs maiden names.

3. Nicknames and most used names.

4. Destiny combinations.

5. Birthdate.

This sequence is based on my experience of what people recognize most readily about their lives. In addition, by starting with the most recognizable traits and moving towards the unknown, more credibility is afforded to the unknown or the yet undiscovered.

One's personal cycle and names are more observable and external than is the nature of the birthdate which reflects the Inner Self. *Our names are what we are, whereas, our birthdate is what we are striving to become.* Some people are deeply in touch with their Inner Self and enjoy a rich, fulfilling life.

People who are not in touch with their inner needs, will not recognize their inner potential and will reflect a proportionate degree of conflict in their life experience. This is an important point to keep in mind when doing an analysis.

Here are some helpful hints to consider when addressing each component of a name analysis:

1. PERSONAL CYCLE

Although a great deal can be said about each cycle year, a comparison of the most recent 3 or 4 years will build a perspective and lend a great deal of credibility to the entire analysis. When comparing several years, remember the following highlights of each of the years. Go back far enough to include a 4, 7, or 9 cycle year.

The highlights are:

1 year Compare the physical energy of the 1 year with the fatigue of the 9 year. Note the impatience of the first 5 months of the 1 year. Emphasize the need to plant seeds and accept new opportunities in June, July, and August.

2 year Note that this year feels like a tea party. It's seems to be all idle chit chat and waiting for everyone else to make up their mind before action can be taken on one's own projects. If major changes were not made in the summer of the 1 year, major changes were forced between January and May of the 2 year.

3 year Emphasize how the year begins with great optimism and ends in great disappointment.

4 year Everyone recognizes this year. Whatever can go wrong, goes wrong — physically, mentally, emotionally, family, friendship, financially, career, home, cars, etc. Remember the

	expression that enough is enough, is enough, already. March and December are the hardest.
5 year	February feels like the sun comes out for the first time since August of the 3 year. Note the difficulty of June and the opportunity to make major life changes in July and August. The 4 year is about survival pains whereas the 5 year is about growth pains.
6 year	Reflect on the endless string of financial obligations.
7 year	Emphasize the first half which is so distinctly disorienting and self-conscious and the terrific desire to quit something in June. Note the second half which simply gets better and better.
8 year	Note the sense of empowerment and the contrast to the self-conscious, disorienting, first 6 months of the 7 year. Any negatives of the 8 year appear in March and April.
9 year	Reflect on the extreme fatigue that begins in January and gets dramatically worse until August. Contrast the low energy and vulnerability of this year to the sense of empowerment experienced in the 8 year. Emphasize the emotions of the 9 year and the temptation to begin new projects in the fall.

2. SURNAMES VERSUS MAIDEN NAMES

Getting married can radically change your life. The change of family name can often point out many of the changes in attitude and experience of life. For example, a woman may grow up in a rigid family where everything has to be planned. She may be attracted to a man who comes from a spontaneous family that loves to party. When the party atmosphere becomes old hat, she may move into a 2rd marriage that is more of a balanced family environment. It's particularly fun when this happens because the comparisons are distinctive and clearly recognizable.

Sometimes people choose mates who have the same family traits. I remember doing an analysis for a woman, let's call her Lesley, who married into a family with the same family combination. I pointed out my inability to compare and contrast the two families because they were the same. She responded by saying, "Yes, I know. I chose him because he was so much like our family, my parents wouldn't object to my marrying him." Once again, the numbers proved their accuracy.

If a man is married, include his wife's maiden name in his analysis. He will recognize the family differences and be more receptive to direct comment about his personal traits.

3. NICKNAMES AND MOST USED NAMES

Remember that all the names have an influence, yet it is the *most used names* that have the greatest impact.

Nicknames are often limited to certain environments such as home or school, or are used only by certain people like grandmother. Describe the qualities of each nickname within the context of where the nickname is used. Describe each nickname independently and don't search out a net resolve of all the nicknames.

4. DESTINY COMBINATIONS

Regardless of the qualities of the given-names, nicknames, and surnames, the **end result of all the names is found in the destiny combination**. It is important to trust this fact and not to down-play the destiny combination because it is less attractive than the given-names and surnames.

5. BIRTHDATE

The birthdate should be analyzed last because it represents the potential of the individual, the Inner Self, the seed of consciousness that is striving to grow back to the source from which it came. Many people are very much out of touch with their inner potential and may fail to recognize their Inner Self. In such a case, they have no sense of their own needs and struggle to find their way in a world defined by everyone else. Their struggle reflects in their life experience and they tend to take on the negative aspects of their name combinations.

OTHER CONSIDERATIONS

A full name analysis can include many other factors such as the full legal name, the business signature, mother's maiden name, changes under the letters, pinnacles and challenges, the first consonant, the first vowel, etc.

A full hour spent on the above list of recommended factors is more than enough for people to digest. Reviewing too many factors simply becomes confusing, watered down, and academic.

PART VI

CHANGING NAMES

CHAPTER 21 — BEFORE YOU CHANGE ANY NAMES

If you are interested in changing your name or anyone else's for that matter, this chapter will be particularly important to you and should be given serious consideration.

Before you change any names, it is imperative to understand the significance of names within the tapestry of conditions that permeate life. How do names compare to the influences of heredity, family-of-origin conditions, the prevailing social, political, and economic environment, education, diet, exercise, etc? How many pieces are there in the puzzle of life and of the total number of pieces, how many pieces do the names represent?

These are very difficult questions to answer in a statistical, factual, "fait accompli" manner. As this book points out, names play a very definite role in the picture of life. Yet, whether they represent the corner stones of the picture, or some of the border pieces, or just some of the internal pieces, is difficult to evaluate. Even though names are a fundamental aspect, there are other vitally important considerations which must be attended to before a change of name will have a valuable impact on one's life.

Before you change your name, it is imperative that you study and address the following topics as they relate to your life:

- **family of origin**
- **family systems theory**
- **dysfunctional families**
- **co-dependency issues**

A book by John Bradshaw called, "Bradshaw: On The Family",

covers all of the above and will direct you to more information if you need it.

If you change your name before you address the above topics, you are more than likely putting a bandaid on festering wounds that have not been dressed.

This point is made strongly because I have repeatedly seen people change their names with great optimism for a better life. Unfortunately, they eventually lose heart and conclude that life doesn't work for them. What they overlook is that a change of name and a million affirmations a day cannot overpower the guilt, shame and anger of unresolved issues stemming from family-of-origin conditions. Everyone must resolve their family-of-origin blueprint before a new future can be successfully built.

CHAPTER 22 — BALANCED NAME COMBINATIONS

A completely balanced name combination must satisfy at least the following conditions:

- the name must draw from a source of energy that is vibrant, dynamic, flexible, creative, and balanced within its own nature. A source energy that is radically independent or overly concerned with peace and harmony is undesirable except in very specific conditions.

- the expression number of the name must be a constructive and encouraging outlet for the source number and move the source energy towards a successful completion of goals.

- the name must offer a constructive and encouraging outlet for the qualities of the Inner Self as identified by the birthdate.

Out of the 81 first name combinations, the 81 surname combinations, and the 81 destiny combinations, there are only a very few combinations that are completely balanced to both inner and outer needs.

Why Do Numbers Count

For women, the first name combinations are 3-3-6 and 6-9-6. When combined with a 6-3-9 surname, they result in the following destiny combinations:

First name		Surname		Destiny
3		6		9
3	+	3	=	6
6		9		6
6		6		3
9	+	3	=	3
6		9		6

For men, the first name combinations are 6-9-6, 6-2-8, and 3-5-8. When combined with a 6-3-9 surname, they result in the following destiny combinations:

First name		Surname		Destiny
6		6		3
9	+	3	=	3
6		9		6
6		6		3
2	+	3	=	5
8		9		8
3		6		9
5	+	3	=	8
8		9		8

In all cases, notice that the surname is a 6-3-9 combination. This is the best possible family name combination for the following reasons:

- the 6-3-9 combination added to any 1 of the 4 most desirable first name combinations, results in a desirable destiny combination. No other surname combination offers this solution.

- the 6-3-9 combination is a desirable family name given that it begins with a source number of a 6 which is accountable, responsible, sensible, congenial, intelligent, plus maternal and paternal in nature. In addition, this combination ends in a 9 which is a quality of letting go, forgiveness, unconditional love, and humanitarian ideals. Within a family context, it is important to give and take for the overall well being of the family unit. Hence, the expression number of 9 supports the harmony of family life.

In contrast, as a first name, the 6-3-9 combination is not as desirable because the individual within the family has to first satisfy his or her own needs before an external focus can be pursued for the greater good of family and community. A stronger, more results oriented first name is desirable to assist one in fulfilling personal needs first before a broader, external focus is pursued.

It is important to note that the combinations for women do not end in an 8 expression number. The qualities of the 8 are strongly focused on material success in an external sense. If a woman focuses too strongly on externals, she will create a conflict with her inherent, internal nature and pay a serious price of pain and discomfort with her internal female organs and her sexual identity. For these reasons, the 3-5-8 and the 6-2-8 combinations are not recommended for women. Not only do they end in an 8, when they are combined with a 6-3-9 surname, they create either a 9-8-8 or a 3-5-8 destiny — even more 8's.

The only desirable destiny for a woman is the 6 if she is interested in a wholesome, mature family setting, good health, success in all walks of life, and the flexibility to be both inspirational and practical. All other destinies have distinctly, undesirable drawbacks for women.

A shortcoming of the 6-9-6 for men and women, or the 6-2-8 for men is the tendency to be overly focused, accountable and responsible. As a result, they sometimes worry excessively which can result in headaches and migraines. They are also prone to being unduly serious and can become a bit stodgy. Yet, out of all the possible combinations, these are amongst the most desirable. Fortunately, the sensible, congenial nature of these combinations tend to prevail.

In comparison, the 3-3-6 combination for women and the 3-5-8 combination for men draw from the source energy of the 3 which is playful, happy, energetic, and loves learning. The 3 embraces the best of the 1, the male energy, and the 2, the female energy. Given that the 3 is the best of both worlds, and that the combinations end in a 6 or an 8, the 3-3-6 for women and the 3-5-8 for men are superb for encouraging a joyful and a successful life.

The 6-2-8 combination is desirable for men focused on business and for those who are intent on being most serious about what they are striving to accomplish. Even so, I often wonder if the same results cannot be acquired by using the lighter and less serious combination of the 3-5-8 for men who are results oriented and have significant material goals.

For the introverted: the 3-3-6 combination is recommended for women and the 3-5-8 combination is recommended for men.

For the extroverted: the 6-9-6 combination is recommended for women and either the 6-9-6 or the 6-2-8 combination is recommended for men.

In the final analysis, the above combinations are the only ones that effectively and holistically embrace the most desirable qualities of mind, body, spirit, and material reality. Although one of the recommended combination may be slightly better than the other, they are all outstanding in comparison to all the other possibilities.

PART VII

SPECIAL TOPICS

CHAPTER 23 — RELATIONSHIPS & COMPATIBILITY

Numerology can be helpful in determining the underlying compatibility between people. The most important factors to consider are:

1. Day of birth
2. Lifepath number
3. Source number of the most used, first name combination
4. Expression number of the destiny combination
5. Personal cycle year

1. THE DAY OF BIRTH

Chapter 11 concluded with a discussion on the physical, mental, and spiritual compatibility groups determined from the day of birth. These groups are:

1-5-7 Physical   2-4-8 Mental   3-6-9 Spiritual

In general terms, these groups form a spectrum from introverted to extroverted with the middle group being a blended/balance point and go-between for the two polarities:

   1-5-7   Introverted
   2-4-8   Blended/Balanced
   3-6-9   Extroverted

People of opposite basic natures (i.e. introverted versus extroverted) do not get along well over an extended period of time. People get along best with those from their same group. The following compatibility considerations apply to each group:

1-5-7   The Physical group gets along best with others in its own group, not well with those in the mental group, and very poorly with those in the spiritual group.

2-4-8   The Mental group gets along best with others in its own group, quite well with those in the spiritual group, and reasonably well with those in the physical group. The mental group are the mediators between the physical and the spiritual groups.

3-6-9   The Spiritual group gets along best with others in its own group, quite well with those in the mental group, and very poorly with those in the physical group.

The compatibility group is the single most important factor in determining long term relationship compatibility. The following considerations also support the importance of the compatibility groups.

The second minor life focus, the day of birth, affects one's life more predominately than do the first or the third minor focus. Just as each of the years in the 9 year cycle grow from a beginning to a peak and then taper off towards the next cycle year, your life is a cycle with a beginning, a middle, and an end. The period from 27 to 54 is the peak of most people's lives when they are the most active.

Where the lifepath number reflects the overall nature of an individual, the second minor life focus (the day of birth) reflects the attitude with which one expresses their overall nature. For example, people can have the same lifepath number, yet be in different compatibility groups. In such a case, they often uphold the same beliefs and values, yet they arrive at the same conclusions from two completely different directions. As a result, it appears that they are always in disagreement when in fact they are not. As the years pass, the amount of discussion required to confirm that they are in agreement becomes a draining, if not depleting, experience. As partners lose their willingness to make the effort to communicate, misunderstandings and resentment build until marriages fail. Unfortunately, during the courtship and early stages of marriage, the inspiration and willingness to accept the other for who they are overshadows the realities of day to day living and people in love are always inspired to believe that it won't happen to them, that they can work it out.

I believe that 70 percent or more of the divorces can be predicted based on the compatibility group factor alone.

2. LIFEPATH

The best way to determine the compatibility of lifepath numbers is to use the same rules as we did for defining compatibility groups. In other words, lifepath numbers of 1-5-7, 2-4-8, and 3-6-9 get along best with lifepath numbers in the same group.

Exceptions to this rule of thumb are:

   2 & 3 because of their cosmopolitan, social nature
   4 & 6 because of their intellectual and home loving nature
   8 & 9 because of their interest in the world overview and service.

3. SOURCE NUMBER OF THE MOST USED, FIRST NAME COMBINATION

The source number of the most used name depicts the individual's fundamental source of thought which is an important consideration for long term compatibility.

The best way to determine the compatibility of the source number of the most used name is to apply the rules of the compatibility group numbers (1-5-7, 2-4-8, 3-6-9). In addition, compatible source numbers are: 2 & 3, 4 & 6, and 8 & 9.

4. EXPRESSION NUMBER OF THE DESTINY COMBINATION

The expression number of the destiny combination depicts the net overall factor that directs one's life. It is the destination at which one will eventually arrive despite all other factors. Obviously, this is an important consideration. Two people can belong to the same group, have compatible goals based on the lifepath number, draw from a similar thought pattern as depicted by the source number of the most used first name, yet, if the final destination is different, somewhere along the way they are going to part ways emotionally, if not physically.

The most compatible numbers in this case can best be determined by applying the rules of the compatibility group numbers (1-5-7, 2-4-8, 3-6-9).

5. PERSONAL CYCLE YEAR

The personal 9 year cycle that each person is in when they meet and when they marry can dramatically affect their experience of compatibility. All the various considerations have been outlined in Chapters 12 and 13.

When two people are in the same cycle year, their experiences in life are chronologically very similar. The similarity of experience generates a deep sense of compassion that often becomes the basis for having a relationship. Unfortunately, many of the other components required to build a long term relationship can be missing. Being in the same cycle year as your partner can be wonderful, but be careful to ensure that there is more foundation to long term relationship than being at the same place at the same time.

CHAPTER 24 — HEALTH CONSIDERATIONS & NUMBERS

Each number is related to a specific part of the physical body and is said to rule that area. An abundance of a given number in the various name combinations and the birthdate will over-emphasize the attention on a given body area. The result will be a sensitivity or a weakness in the respective area. The following overview describes how and why each number governs one or more areas of the body.

ONE

The one rules the head. Like Aries, the one is focused on developing a persona, a sense of self. They are striving to individuate, to become independent and be their own person. A sense of self is an intellectual construct, a mental perspective, hence the focus of the one is on the head. Ones often have eye, ear, nose, and sinus problems. When they catch a common cold, it settles in their head. Although they are subject to baldness, they often have an abundance of body hair.

TWO

The two is related to the emotions of life, the fluids, and the feminine principal — menstruation, conception, and birth. As a result, an over emphasis of two will affect the reproductive system of women.

The two rules the kidneys which are responsible for cleansing the blood stream, the basic fluid of the body. Weak kidneys can cause water retention in the body and a tendency to readily gain weight. Because the kidneys are directly related to the bladder, twos often have weak bladders and make frequent trips to the bathroom. The gentle, easygoing, lack-of-action nature of twos manifests in poor circulation of their blood. Consequently, they suffer from cold hands and feet. Varicose veins are a common problem for them.

The two is also related to the sense of taste which can be distorted when the two is imbalanced.

THREE

The three rules the liver which is the largest organ of the body and performs many functions — all of which are vital to our aliveness, hence the "live-r". Thousands of chemical reactions take place in it every second during life. When healthy, it inactivates hormones no longer needed, synthesizes many amino acids used in building tissues. It breaks proteins into sugar and fat when required for energy or eaten in excess. The liver also produces lecithin, cholesterol, bile, and blood albumin, vital to the removal of tissue waste. It produces prothrombin essential to the clotting of the blood, and enumerable enzymes and coenzymes. It converts sugar into body starch or glycogen, stores it, and reconverts it to sugar when needed. And it stores iron, copper, and several trace minerals, vitamin A, and to some extent D, E, K, and the B vitamins. Last, a healthy liver destroys harmful substances such as histamine and detoxifies drugs, poisons, chemicals, and toxins from bacterial infections. An imbalance of three will affect the functioning of the liver and undermine one's sense of aliveness and vitality.

In addition, because threes are extroverts, their health disorders will show externally in the form of skin problems — rashes, eczema, and skin cancer. The three is also related to the sense of smell which can be distorted when the three is imbalanced.

FOUR

The four rules the intestines which are related to our ability to digest and absorb the nutrients of our food. The intestines essentially perform the same function as the root system of the plant. They must precisely absorb what is healthy and eliminate what is not desirable. Fours are also subject to boils when the intestines absorb more toxins than they should.

Because the four has a tendency to hang on and not let go, they are subject to constipation and bloating about the waistline, buttocks, and thighs.

The fourth physical sense is hearing. As a consequence, fours have either perfect hearing or a tin-ear.

FIVE

The five rules the stomach. When they are wound-up or excited, they have a difficult time eating or holding their food down. Because the five is a very intense, dynamic quality, they often suffer from a knot in their stomach, a feeling of a turn-key that wants to explode. Their nervous stomachs are often diagnosed as ulcerated.

In addition, the fifth physical sense is that of sight. The combination of a sensitive stomach and a discerning eye, results in the fives experience of not being able "to stomach the sight of their food" unless it is presented just right. Their intuitive, insightful nature often sees more than they want to see. Because seeing, like hearing, is selective, they can suffer from poor eyesight. They will choose to ignore what they can see so they will not have to deal with the more harsh aspects of life. In this sense, they can close themselves off from life and opt for the bliss of ignorance.

SIX

The six rules the womb which is related to budding, procreation, paternal, and maternal instincts. The six has a great love for home, family, and community. It is very common for "confirmed-bachelors" to unexpectedly marry in a six cycle year or for women to find themselves in the family way.

The sixth sense is mind and is related to accountability and responsibility. Those who take on too much responsibility and worry excessively are subject to migraine headaches. Although this is a tendency of the six, their stable, sensible nature seldom falls pray to this weakness.

SEVEN

The seven rules the lungs which are directly related to the breath of life. As the mystic, the poet, and the philosopher, sevens are etherial by nature and deeply in touch with the spirit of life which is directly related to the words inspiration, respiration, and expiration. These words share a common root derivation.

> "In-spiration" means to dwell in the spirit of life.
> "Re-spiration" means to breath-in, to re-spirit the body.
> "Ex-piration" means to breath-out, to exit-the-spirit.

When a seven catches a common cold, it will settle in their lungs whereas a one will get a head cold. Sevens are subject to pneumonia and pleurisy. Their delicate nature and sensitive lungs reflect in a need for more than an average amount of sleep.

EIGHT

The eight rules the genitals, the basis of the reproductive and procreative systems. In addition, the eight is focused on material success which is an external focus and in opposition to the internal female energies and female sexuality. As a consequence, women with an abundance of eight in their names are very prone to reproductive system disorders and suffer with difficult menstrual cycles. Generally males cope more harmoniously with the external, material focus of the eight and are not as receptive to genital disorders as are women who have an abundance of eights in their nature.

NINE

The nine rules the nervous system. In order to be our complete and full selves in physical reality, we must be fully receptive and in tune with all life. Since our nervous system is our antenna, it must be complete and finely tuned to embrace the full spectrum of life. Hence, nines are deeply feeling, compassionate, and very inspired. Nines can suffer from all manner of nervous system disorders if they do not stay centered and balanced. When their nervous systems are overly sensitive, their efforts are scattered and their nature becomes flighty and ungrounded.

CHAPTER 25 — BUSINESS MANAGEMENT, MONEY & YOU

To begin this chapter, let me give you a brief perspective of my business experience. In 1972, I was one of two founding partners of a data processing company that for 15 years was know as the accountant's accountant in Canada. Before the advent of the mini-computer, we offered computer services to professional accountants. From six offices across the country, we processed their client's general ledgers, accounts receivable, accounts payable, and personal tax returns. During our peak seasons, we would employ over 400 people.

In my experience, the principles of numerology have a number of direct applications to business management including:

- the choice of business and product names
- identifying personality profiles
- confirming aptitude evaluations
- choosing office addresses
- determining the impact of the 9 Year Cycle

Of the above, the most poignant business tool is understanding the impact of the 9 Year Cycle on personal and corporate goals. To my chagrin, my greatest losses have come when I decided to ignore cyclic wisdom. Conversely, my greatest successes came when I allowed the creative tension of the cycles to build and I made my decisions with the odds heavily stacked in my favour.

9 YEAR CYCLE

Consider the following scenario. After a very long search, you have found just the right man for the job. His education, experience, and goals align perfectly with you and your company. Not only can you afford him, you have an expanding carrier path available that will secure his interest for the long term. You've checked his references and you are enthralled with his aptitude and personality profiles. It's a perfect match, so you hire him. He begins work but can't seem to get on the right foot even after several months of breaking into his new position. A year later, you part company, both disappointed that it hadn't gone as planned.

From both an employer and an employee's perspective, beginning a new job can be likened to dancing. Have you ever started a dance on the wrong foot and stopped to begin again only to miss the beat or have your partner start on the wrong foot? Sometimes you bite the bullet and acknowledge this simply isn't your song and you sit that one out. Other times, you may bear with it until it works. Yet, in this case, have you ever noticed that the rest of the dance is never as satisfying as one that began on the right foot?

The key to dancing lies in the timing. In the larger picture of life, the timing is determined by the 9 Year Cycle. Even though your new man has everything going for him, is he in the right season to begin a new job? To help answer that question, Appendix 'C' offers a detailed table that outlining the probability of success for each month of the entire 9 Year Cycle.

A further complication to the cycles comes with blending your cycle with someone elses. Let's refer back to the example of the right man for the job with the complication that he is in an adverse cycle. Let's add to the plot that you are in a superb cyclic period and you hire him regardless of his cycle. Although it is unlikely, he may fulfill your every expectation. Unfortunately, based on his own experience of his cycle, he will not feel good about himself and the job he is doing. After some months or a year, he resigns, leaving you to begin your search all over again.

If a company is more than five years old and has a reasonable number of employees, it will have taken on a life of its own. When this is so, a great deal of attention must be given to the company's cycle which is computed from the date of incorporation. Add the month and day of incorporation to the current year plus one to compute the current cycle year of the company. When a company has taken on a life of its own, major corporate decisions should be made in light of the corporate cycle for the best overall results. Regardless of the corporate needs and cycle, for an individual beginning a major new project or starting new with the company, the individual's personal cycle must be given full consideration. Each employee must be on the right foot and in tune with the corporate rhythm to materialize successful conclusions of corporate objectives.

BUSINESS & PRODUCT NAMES

When you are beginning a new business or naming a new product, you may as well test the theory of numerology and add all the zest you can to your new venture. If there is nothing to numerology, you have nothing to lose. If there is power in the symbology of words, you have much to gain. Assuming, of course, that you choose the appropriate name. So, what are the rules?

First, choose names that are completely balanced combinations. For your reference, they are: 3-5-8, 6-2-8, 6-9-6, and 3-3-6. The descriptions presented in Chapter 17 can be applied to business and product names.

You may wish to go beyond the boundaries of these combinations for specific reasons. For example, you may have a product that is specifically female oriented and you want a gentle, soft ambience to represent its mood. In this case, a 2-4-6 or a 2-6-8 combination may feel appropriate. If you are dealing with outdoor products to do with nature, possibly a 7-1-8 combination could be considered — but be cautious with employing 7's.

Under no circumstances should you use an 8-9-8 combination. It has too much impact and inevitably will draw unscrupulous people and events to your business world. Do not be tempted to use this combination.

As with personal names, the corporate and product names that are verbally used, will have the greatest impact. This can create a complication when the name of your company is different from the name used to answer the phone. Or, when the name on the corporate letterhead is different from the name by which your company is known. Strive to use one of the completely balanced combinations for answering the telephone and settle for one of the topnotch but slightly less than ideal combinations for the full corporate name. Some of these combinations are: 1-5-6, 2-4-6, 5-1-6, 7-8-6, 9-6-6, 2-6-8, 5-3-8, 7-1-8, 9-8-8. That's all of them baring 1-7-8 which should only be used with extreme caution.

Finding a business name or a product name that sounds good, makes sense, hasn't been used, meets government approval, and has the right numbers, can be nigh onto impossible. Other times, the perfect name appears like magic. Good luck stalking the perfect name with the right numbers. Certainly a computer program can be most helpful when reviewing the endless possibilities.

PERSONALITY PROFILES & APTITUDE EVALUATIONS

It has been my experience that the executives of companies who are proficient with numerology continue to use conventional personality and aptitude tests as corporate policy. They use the numerological insights to confirm the test results and their own instinctual hunch about the potential candidate.

The true value of numerology can come to the fore over a business luncheon or supper, when those proficient with numerology, can compute combinations in their head. Insights are immediate in comparison to formal testing.

As many and as poignant as the insights of names and birthdates are, I refer once again to the value of simply knowing the personal cycle of your client or your perspective employee. For this calculation, you simply need their month and day of birth. If you ask for their full birthdate, it will raise suspicions. A simple way to acquire the needed information is casually ask if they are a Virgo. Most people will think nothing of correcting you if you have guessed wrong. "Oh, Taurus. What day in April is that?" Now you know their personal cyclic year because you simply need to add their month and day of birth to the current year plus one. Then comes the hard part — will you listen to the insight that the cycle offers?

BUSINESS ADDRESSES

The influence of a business or house address is determined by the following sequence, beginning with the most personal or immediate factor and growing towards the collective overview: suite number, street number, street name, city name, country name.

For an example, let's begin with the collective and work down to the personal experience within the collective. The national characteristics and personality of Americans is different from Germans. Within America, each city and town has its own character as does the street on which you live. If you live in an apartment building at a given address, your experience within the nature of your building will be influenced by your apartment number. If you like a particular building on a given street, the most important factor becomes choosing the apartment number.

If you are about to purchase a home or to relocate your office, the best number for a house is a 6 and for an office an 8. Nothing else is really suitable other than a 6 for the office number. This, of course, means reducing the address numbers to a single digit such as 1700 ABC Street to an 8.

If you own your own home or office building and want to change the address, you can apply to the city, providing there are suitable numbers available between your house and the next. If you are able to make a change, be patient and allow some months or a year or two for the new numbers to have impact. Remember that you and your family, or your office staff, have more influence than the address number. Yet, the address is part of the puzzle and does have impact.

As for telephone numbers, I have never been able to give them any more attention than how easy are they to remember — although I do not doubt that the same principles still apply.

LOTTERY NUMBERS

There are two ways to play lottery numbers. Pick numbers at random and hope to get lucky or carefully choose a specific set of numbers and play them consistently. I personally like the latter approach which suggests that I am creating my own reality. When my numbers come up, I believe that I drew that money to me by my conscious choice.

What numbers should you choose? Integrity and personal power blossom when we are aligned with our true, spiritual essence. From this perspective, your overall most lucky number is your lifepath number which is in harmony with your Inner Self. Using this number is to call forth and evoke your personal highest good.

For a 649 lottery, use the numbers of your birthdate. Because your birthdate does not include enough numbers, add a few of your favourite numbers or ones that simply look good with your birthdate. Now compute the single digit. Does it equal your lifepath number? If not, change the least significant number in the sequence to generate your lifepath number. Now you have your sequence, stick with it and let it build an identity, a vortex of power large enough to attract the results you desire. Don't expect results overnight — you need lots of faith and conviction to win the lottery game.

IN CONCLUSION

Congratulations, you have survived and are now in the position to compute name combinations, lifepaths, and cycles. Undoubtedly, you have already discovered many fascinating insights into your friends and family. As you practice, the more insightful you will become. I hope that your new skills will enhance your awareness and your appreciation of life.

If you have read this book because you are interested in changing your name and you cannot find one that satisfies you, contact me by way of my publisher and I can send you an exhaustive list of first names and surnames that will meet your needs. Or, you could purchase my book, **NAMING YOUR CHILD,** which also has a complete list of balanced first names.

As a parting gesture, let us pause for a moment and consider the number 30 as used by those modern communicators, journalists. Around the world, from the ancient, hot-lead newsrooms of China to the cold-type, high-tech newsrooms of Japan and America, the number 30 is used many thousands of times a day. Why?

Time-honoured tradition. The number 30, written — 30 —, appears on headstones of departed reporters and editors. It appears in in-house journalism magazines to signify who has just passed away. It's used on cakes when journalists retire. It's part of the parlance heard at reporters' watering holes around the world. To go "30" or become "30" has dire connotations understood only by newsmen and newswomen.

The number — 30 — has appeared for almost 200 years at the end of the story. It means there *ain't* no more. This is the last page of the story. Finito! It's origins are lost in the annals of the first continental telegraph companies, when stories were wired to newspapers one small page at a time. In the old days of newsgathering, before the coming of the telephone and teletype, reporters gave their hastily written stories to telegraph operators who tapped them out in Morris Code to the telegraph office around the corner from the newspaper. Stories were longer back then, so it was not uncommon for operators to break a long story into several "takes", or single-page bursts. At the other end, however, the story would be transcribed by another harassed operator in an office with thousands of pieces of paper milling around. How to keep the story straight? Easy. After each "take", the operator would type — MORE —, or — MTC — (more to come). Each page was given a number.

But when the last bit of the story was sent, the operator signed off with — 30 —. Inside the newsroom, the practice caught on, and today all stories moving on wires or produced by local reporters end the same way. It's fascinating to see wire copy moving from Tass in Moscow in the Russian alphabet to a member in Beijing, where it is translated into Chinese. The only thing they will have in common is — 30 — following the last word.

To modern journalists, the number 30 is a reminder of the past, a legacy from the forerunners of their craft. Over the years, any attempt to dump — 30 — into the trash heap has been put down or laughed off by editors around the world. Thirty continues to be with a working journalist all their life, from the end of their first story to the beginning of their last story on earth. It is a badge of recognition that can be found on coats, pins, bar glasses, and even worked into the motif of press clubs around the world.

That's the whole story and it's time to simply say:

$$— 30 —$$

APPENDIX "A" — THE EVOLUTION OF THE ZODIAC SIGNS

One day, the spirit of Aries awoke with a start to find himself trapped in a human body. He leaped out of bed and with great vigour began to explore his physical boundaries. He was so wrapped up in his exploration that he was oblivious to the presence of anyone else until one day he bumped into Taurus.

Taurus said, "Excuse me Aries, but your not the only one on this space ship called Earth. You need to become aware of other people, of the duality of life, and to learn about feelings." Aries just shrugged while Taurus continued to sense and feel her environment. How she loved the smells of the earth, the beauty of the flowers, and the caress of the wind. She felt so connected to everything that it was very easy for her to just sit there and be.

But the quiet and peacefulness didn't last for long when in a rather loud voice, Gemini enthusiastically exclaims, "This is exciting! Here we are! We're in these neat things called bodies. And there are a bunch of us. Let's figure it all out!" And so Gemini started to ask questions about everything imaginable. There was so much to investigate that he only had time to ask a few questions about this, and a few about that.

While Gemini was flitting all over the place, Cancer pipes up with, "Wait a minute Gemini! This isn't as simple as your making it out to be. We have to look deeper. We need to get organized and to build homes for everyone. And your forgetting about the feelings that Taurus is experiencing but is too shy to talk about." And so Cancer starts to ask much deeper questions. She collects and saves everything she can. One day, when she has enough information, she will be able to figure it all out. Cancer explores everything in great detail by sending out feelers, like fine roots, to investigate her environment. In this sense, she is very aware of Taurus' feelings. In fact, she feels even more than Taurus does but she is so busy analyzing her data and looking after everyone else that she seldom takes the time to talk about her own feelings.

Unable to contain himself for a moment longer, Leo interjects, "Wait a minute everyone — hold it! Look at me! It's pretty obvious that we each have a body, feelings, a mind, and a place to live. What we need now is some pizzazz. We need to develop a personality. We need to put ourselves out in the world and to use all of our talents." With some hesitation, the other signs ask, "That sounds pretty good Leo, but how do we do it?" With a flair, Leo answers, "I don't know, but I believe I have enough courage to try. I'm a bit uncertain though. And if I do try, you had better acknowledge me, or I'll get really mad." Bravely putting all doubts aside, Leo steps onto a stage and begins to promote some very interesting, new ideas about life and love and children. He talks with conviction and determination. Leo insists that Gemini has asked enough questions and Cancer has done enough organizing. What is needed now is action, a willingness to explore new horizons, to develop new products, give birth to new ideas, be progressive, dynamic, take a risk, just do it and let the chips fall where they may. None of the other signs seem to be too convinced, but Leo pays them no heed and continues with his promotional speech.

Wow, is he fired up or what! Where is he getting these creative new ideas from anyway? He's acting like he has all of the answers, and he's getting a bit bossy. The other signs start to shuffle their feet as they become progressively more restless. Leo stops in the middle of a sentence and demands to know what is wrong. "Come on!", says Leo, "Why aren't you supporting me? I said you had to acknowledge me if I did this. Well?" With some reluctance, the other signs stammer, "Ahh, you sure have lots of energy, Leo. And you made some good points." Obviously perturbed, Leo retorts with, "Some good points! Hah, all my points were terrific!"

Knowing that Leo is about to get rather angry, Virgo steps onto the stage and says, "Now wait a minute Leo. Your points are excellent but your taking this too personally. I've watched each one of you and I can see where everyone plays an important role. I know how to fix this confusion and I know exactly how life should work. We simply need to go a little deeper in a conceptual sense. What you need is some feedback and some good advice." With a critical tone, Virgo proceeds to tell Aries to sit still — that he had his turn. She tells Taurus to put down her flowers and to listen up. And she tells Gemini to stop asking questions when she already knows the answers. To Cancer, Virgo says, "Stop crying just because you think Leo wasn't acknowledged and had his feelings hurt. Leo's only trying to inspire us." Then she turns to Leo and again tells him that his points were terrific but he needs to let other people talk too. Virgo told Leo, "You need to understand that your not the only star in this movie called life." She insisted that everyone be responsible and that everything be very tidy without any loose ends. All of the signs were impressed with Virgo's intelligence and innate sense of knowing. By the time Virgo was finished giving directions, they each had a very clear sense of how they should behave — that is, until Libra pipes up.

"What now?", cry the first six signs. With great diplomacy, Libra complements each of them and especially Virgo for her insights. Carefully, Libra goes on to acknowledge that they have gained a good sense of how physical life works, but now they need to look at the more subtle, spiritual aspects of life. Libra continues to explain that the true mysteries of life are to be found in relationship to each other. Libra is very clear that being intimate, open, and receptive is what life is all about and he encourages everyone to pursue relationships. Libra looks a bit sensitive to the other signs, and it feels like he is missing part of the story. Yet, it did sound very appealing to seek the spiritual purpose of life, so everyone began to cultivate and explore relationships.

Within all the new relationships, many personal sacrifices were made, which secretly bothered everyone. Unfortunately, no one really said so as they made an all out effort to be unconditional and supportive. Sometimes it seemed that the harder they tried, the more difficult the relationships became. Many strange struggles ensued until one day Scorpio had had enough and sharply interjected that relationships can only work when people remember the duality of life. Scorpio was very determined that Libra's idea of oneness within relationship was too idealistic. She insisted that the value of relationship lies in the differences. That, once again, everyone had to look deeper, and remember that life on planet earth stems from sexual energy, that relationships are a composite of two individuals who had to continue to clearly honour themselves for their unique identity. Scorpio talked with great authority which took the breath away form most of the signs and left them feeling a bit frightened.

All of a sudden there were gales of laughter from the back of the crowd and Sagittarius boldly strolled up to Scorpio and addressed the signs. "Scorpio is right", he said, "But everyone here is being far too serious. You need to play and laugh more. It's great to be in relationship and it's great to honour your sexuality and your differences, but there is a bigger picture to understand. You guys are too funny for words. Come with me and I'll not only show you a whole world that you haven't seen, I'll show you many worlds, and we'll have lots of fun along the way." As Sagittarius started to jog across the meadow, everyone shrugged, smiled, and ran after Sagittarius because — he — he really seemed to know what he was doing. It was like — he had integrated everything they were all talking about, and he seemed to be very happy.

After Sagittarius had taught them much about their world and about the sciences, he introduced them to Capricorn. He explained that Capricorn was his teacher. He suggested that they should listen carefully to Capricorn because she was exceptionally wise and had many insights into the future. They were told that throughout the land, Capricorn was acclaimed to be a great leader of people.

One day, Capricorn admitted that much of her insight came from a very strange sign who was totally different from all the other signs. This sign dressed differently and, in fact, did almost everything differently than everyone else. His name was Aquarius. Not many people knew Aquarius because he kept pretty much to himself. Apparently, Aquarius preferred to stay alone because he feared becoming like the other signs. Strangely enough, Aquarius was also very concerned that he would be rejected by everyone for being so different. None of them quite understood that paradox.

And then one day, Capricorn told them the most amazing story about yet another sign called Pisces who was the dreamer of dreams. Pisces was apparently very sensitive and often didn't have words for what she was feeling. Her only real friend was Aquarius, although it was a strange relationship. They were friends because Aquarius liked Pisces' dreams and would try to live what Pisces dreamt. This was very hard for Aquarius because Pisces was never very clear about much of anything, except when she danced. Once Aquarius could do the things that Pisces dreamt about, he would seek out Capricorn and tell her about his latest experiment. In Capricorn's wisdom, she knew that Pisces and Aquarius were God's messengers and her responsibility was to lead the world to a brighter future based on the divine guidance that came to her by way of Pisces and Aquarius.

Stillness filled the air as the signs reflected on the intricate design of life. Each sign had learned from the other and they had come to realize that each of them brought a gift to life. That none of them were less important than the other. What a wonderful journey of discovery they had shared. Each time they thought they had the answer, there was another sign to meet, and more to learn. No one said it out loud, but everyone wondered if there wasn't a 13th sign.

Well now, that's a story for another day.

by Lance Shaler © 2010

APPENDIX "B" — SUMMARY OF METAPHORS & KEYWORDS

A summary of the metaphors and keywords used to create word pictures of the qualities of the numbers. See the following page for

PLANT	HUMAN	SENSES	ASTRO*	BODY	KEYWORD
1. Seed	Male	Touch	Aries	Head	Pioneer
2. Sprouting	Female	Taste	Taurus	Kidneys	Diplomat
3. First Leaf	Child	Smell	Gemini	Liver	Extrovert
4. Roots	Student	Hearing	Cancer	Intestines	Analyzer
5. Rapid Growth	Traveller	Sight	Leo	Stomach	Promoter
6. Budding	Family	Mind	Virgo	Womb	Counsellor
7. Blossom	Phil*	Spirit	Libra	Lungs	Introvert
8. Ripe Apple	Admin*	Grounding	Scorpio	Genitals	Justice
9. Apple Drops	Teacher	Full-Self	Sagittarius	Nervous System	Humanitarian

Astro* = Astrology

Phil* = Philosopher

Admin* = Administrator

Why Do Numbers Count

A summary of the qualities from a visual perspective:

Why Do Numbers Count

Page 276

APPENDIX "C" — PROBABILITIES OF SUCCESS

The following table depicts the probability of success for beginning new projects that are one or more years in duration. Shorter term projects such as day to day survival need attention regardless of the theoretical cycle of the day.

The percentage numbers under the category of 'Probability of Success' reflect the probability of realizing a successful conclusion to projects begun during the respective time frames. In my opinion, a percentage of less than 70 is a poor bet in any kind of business or personal venture. On the other hand, anything over 80% is outstanding although nothing is guaranteed even in the category of Ideal which suggests that the probability is from 95-99%. Even the highest of probabilities does not replace the need to apply common sense and good business management.

CYCLE YEAR	TIME PERIOD	PROBABILITY OF SUCCESS	(%)
1	Jan 1 to Jan 31	Unlikely	20-29
	Feb 1 to Feb 28	Poor	30-39
	Mar 1 to Mar 31	Weak	40-49
	Apr 1 to Apr 30	Fair	50-59
	May 1 to May 31	Good	60-69
	Jun 1 to Jun 18	Excellent	70-79
	Jun 19 to Jul 31	Ideal	95-99
	Aug 1 to Aug 17	Outstanding	80-94
	Aug 18 to Aug 31	Good	60-69
	Sep 1 to Oct 31	Weak	40-49
	Nov 1 to Dec 31	Excellent	70-79

Why Do Numbers Count

CYCLE YEAR	TIME PERIOD	PROBABILITY OF SUCCESS	(%)
2	Jan 1 to Feb 28	Excellent	70-79
	Mar 1 to Mar 31	Good	60-69
	Apr 1 to Apr 30	Outstanding	80-94
	May 1 to Jun 19	Excellent	70-79
	Jun 20 to Jul 31	Fair	50-59
	Aug 1 to Aug 18	Excellent	70-79
	Aug 19 to Sep 30	Fair	50-59
	Oct 1 to Oct 31	Good	60-69
	Nov 1 to Dec 31	Excellent	70-79
3	Jan 1 to Apr 17	Excellent	70-79
	Apr 18 to May 31	Fair	50-59
	Jun 1 to Jul 18	Excellent	70-79
	Jul 19 to Aug 31	Weak	40-49
	Sep 1 to Sep 30	Fair	50-59
	Oct 1 to Nov 30	Weak	40-49
	Dec 1 to Dec 31	Fair	50-59
4	Jan 1 to Feb 13	Weak	40-49
	Feb 14 to Feb 28	Poor	30-39
	Mar 1 to Mar 31	Impossible	0-19
	Apr 1 to Apr 30	Fair	50-59
	May 1 to May 31	Weak	40-49
	Jun 1 to Aug 31	Poor	30-39
	Sep 1 to Oct 31	Fair	50-59
	Nov 1 to Nov 19	Weak	40-49
	Nov 20 to Nov 31	Poor	30-39
	Dec 1 to Dec 31	Unlikely	20-29
5	Jan 1 to Jan 31	Poor	30-39
	Feb 1 to Feb 28	Weak	40-49
	Mar 1 to May 18	Fair	50-59
	May 19 to May 31	Weak	40-49
	Jun 1 to Jun 30	Unlikely	20-29
	Jul 1 to Aug 31	Ideal	95-99
	Sep 1 to Sep 30	Excellent	70-79
	Oct 1 to Nov 30	Fair	50-59
	Dec 1 to Dec 31	Excellent	70-79

Why Do Numbers Count

CYCLE YEAR	TIME PERIOD	PROBABILITY OF SUCCESS	(%)
6	Jan 1 to Mar 31	Excellent	70-79
	Apr 1 to May 31	Fair	50-59
	Jun 1 to Jul 18	Excellent	70-79
	Jul 19 to Jul 31	Fair	50-59
	Aug 1 to Aug 31	Weak	40-49
	Sep 1 to Sep 30	Excellent	70-79
	Oct 1 to Nov 30	Good	60-69
	Dec 1 to Dec 31	Fair	50-59
7	Jan 1 to Jan 31	Fair	50-59
	Feb 1 to Apr 30	Weak	40-49
	May 1 to May 31	Poor	30-39
	Jun 1 to Jun 30	Unlikely	20-29
	Jul 1 to Jul 17	Fair	50-59
	Jul 18 to Aug 31	Outstanding	80-94
	Sep 1 to Sep 18	Fair	50-59
	Sep 19 to Dec 31	Excellent	70-79
8	Jan 1 to Feb 28	Outstanding	80-94
	Mar 1 to Mar 17	Fair	50-59
	Mar 18 to Apr 30	Unlikely	20-29
	May 1 to Jul 17	Excellent	70-79
	Jul 18 to Aug 31	Outstanding	80-94
	Sep 1 to Nov 30	Excellent	70-79
	Dec 1 to Dec 31	Good	60-69
9	Jan 1 to Jan 15	Fair	50-59
	Jan 16 to Jun 30	Poor	30-39
	Jul 1 to Jul 31	Impossible	0-19
	Aug 1 to Sep 30	Poor	30-39
	Oct 1 to Dec 31	Unlikely	**20-29

** Do not be fooled by the attractiveness of the conditions during this time frame. Refer to Chapter 13 for a detailed description of this period.

DISCOVER FOR YOURSELF

✓ Why only some relationships work?

✓ How compatible am I to my mate, the person I'm dating or others?

✓ Why are our children so different from each other?

✓ Why do some children co-operate and others antagonize parents & teachers?

✓ Why do I have "good days" & "bad days"?

✓ Can I predict when I should make major purchases?

✓ Do numbers affect my health?

✓ Can I optimize my happiness?

www.ingramcontent.com/pod-product-compliance
Lightning Source LLC
Chambersburg PA
CBHW031642170426
43195CB00035B/291